THE DICTIONARY OF EVEN MORE DISEASED ENGLISH

The Dictionary of Even More Diseased English

Kenneth Hudson

MACMILLAN PRESS
LONDON

Macmillan Reference Books

First published 1983 by

THE MACMILLAN PRESS LTD
London and Basingstoke
Associated Companies throughout the world

British Library Cataloguing in Publication Data

Hudson, Kenneth
    The dictionary of even more diseased English.
    1. English language — Dictionaries
    I. Title
    423   PE1625

ISBN 0-333-34170-8

Typeset by Leaper & Gard Ltd, Bristol
Printed in Hong Kong

Contents

The man who understood the problem

'I look with pleasure upon my book, however defective, and deliver it to the world with the spirit of a man that has endeavoured well. That it will immediately become popular I have not promised to myself: a few wild blunders, and risible absurdities, from which no work of such multiplicity was ever free, may for a time furnish folly with laughter, and harden ignorance in contempt; but useful diligence will at last prevail and there can never be wanting some who distinguish desert; who will consider that no dictionary of a living tongue ever can be perfect, since, while it is hastening to publication, some words are budding, and some falling away.'

Samuel Johnson: Preface to *Dictionary*, 1755

Introduction

The Dictionary of Diseased English was published in 1977 and since then it has been twice reprinted. During these six years there has been a constant and most welcome flow of letters from total strangers all over the world, congratulating, fulminating, nit-picking, correcting and suggesting. I have been reminded once again that the main value of a book lies not in the material presented within its covers but in its extraordinary power to unlock other people's minds and hearts, so that one receives, absolutely free, a stack of information which one would have obtained in no other way and which, carefully filed away and preserved, can form the basis of one's further writings on the subject. The facts and opinions one needs are scattered over six continents, frequently in the most unlikely places. The problem is to get at them and nothing achieves this as successfully and rapidly as a book to which people can respond. There is no point in delaying publication until one knows everything. That day will never come. There is no point, either, in developing a neurosis about criticism. The most useful additions to one's knowledge are often contained in an abusive letter which minces no words in calling one an ignorant fool. This is known in academic circles as the community of scholars.

Unfortunately, however, a number of my correspondents had not understood what I was trying to do and, since the present book takes over where *The Dictionary of Diseased English* left off, it seems helpful to spell this out once again. In 1977 I offered a definition of 'Diseased English' which, so far as I am concerned, has stood the test of time and I can do no better than repeat it here. It is 'English which, either deliberately or unconsciously, is used with so serious a lack of precision that it ceases to be an effective means of communication and serves only to confuse or mislead'.

There is an important difference between 'Diseased English' and misused English. No great harm is done by the gardening enthusiast who says 'concubine' when he means 'columbine', by the police witness who says that the accused was 'proceeding at a fast speed', or by the person who reveals that he has 'proffered his resignation', as if it were a glass of sherry on a tray. The split infinitive, too, is not likely to bring the end of the world any closer, although a number of my correspondents would disagree with me. What should be exposed, fought and ridiculed at every possible opportunity is pompous rubbish which attempts to give simple, everyday affairs an importance which they in no way deserve and which constitutes a form of verbal fraud to which more or less innocent people are being exposed day in, day out.

In *The Dictionary of Diseased English* I brought a number of categories of people to court as particularly persistent offenders. They included specialists in psychology, psychiatry, the social sciences, business management, education, wine, tourism, entertainment, food and the arts. All these, I suggested, frequently find themselves in the unfortunate position of having nothing to say, but of being obliged to conceal the fact as best they can. They are wordmongers, in the sense that mere words are all they have to offer. For them, the medium is indeed the message. People with a genuine piece of information can usually manage to convey it in an acceptably straightforward and intelligible way. 'The verbal nonsense', I wrote, 'tends to come from people with nothing to say, but with a powerful vested interest in saying it impressively'. Or, in even plainer terms, from people with a living to earn and a career to further.

In *The Dictionary of Diseased English* and in two other books published soon afterwards, *The Jargon of the Professions* (1978) and *The Language of Modern Politics* (1978), I tried as hard as I could to explain that I was not an opponent of anybody's technical language, nor was I trying to resist linguistic change. Technical expressions are frequently necessary. Without them one cannot think, cannot discuss. And no-one in his right mind would attempt to play King Canute with English, to fossilize it. But there is good technical language, the tool of specialist communication, and bad technical language, the masonic glue which serves only to bind one member of a profession to another. Equally, there is good change, which keeps the language alive and allows new moods and expressions to be expressed, and bad change, which simply debases words and makes them no longer capable of helping one person to understand another. Bad technical language and bad change add up to diseased language, or nearly so, the qualification being that language is not just a matter of individual words or expressions, but sounds which indicate that the intellect and the emotions are at work. Once the disease has set in, the longer the passage, the more serious the condition of the patient.

In the following passage, the two patients are almost beyond hope. Even the best of doctors can do little for them. The cancer has spread to every cell of their bodies. This happens to come from an article on 'The Psychology of Strikes', an interesting and important subject, but its puffed-wheat, more-air-than-nutriment style is typical of much that is written nowadays. It is not only diseased, but highly infectious. The two patients should be allowed absolutely no visitors at all:

> 'It was hypothesized that the attitudinal militancy of local officers would be organised according to superordinate cognitive dimensions. More specifically, following the work of Thomas (1976) and Walton and McKersie (1965), the two dimensions which best describe attitudinal militancy were expected to be distributive and integrative dimensions. The distributive dimension differentiates issues involving conflict of interest and underlies the win-lose (zero-sum joint outcome space) component of issues (Thomas, 1976). The integrative dimension differentiates issues involving concern for the welfare of others (Ruble and Thomas, 1976). In resolving distributive issues, the resolution involves division of finite resources, and the major decision criterion is increasing as much as possible the party's satisfaction under the condition that the employment relationships are sustained and prolonged. In resolving integrative issues, the resolution involves increasing the joint benefits accruing to the parties and the major decision criteria is the overall quality of the resolution.'[1]

Many of my correspondents have been anxious to supply extracts from their private collections of such horrors and I am deeply grateful to them. Dr Francis Hayes, of the University of Florida, believes that an international body of people he calls 'the amateur Freudians' are particularly dangerous, with their self-indulgent use of libido, id, ego, superego, manic depressive, paranoia, peer group, pleasure principle, penis envy, and the rest. His wrath has boiled up in an article splendidly titled 'The Great Dismal Swamp of Amateur Freudian Literary Criticism'.[2] This contains a strong attack on what has been done to and with the term 'complex'. 'Complex,' writes Dr Hayes, 'may, often does, turn the palpably not-true into phrases that smell as they disarm'.[3] A great deal of today's language does, in fact, 'smell as it disarms' — the phrase is an

---

[1] Nigel Nicholson and John Kelly: 'The Psychology of Strikes', *Journal of Occupational Behaviour*, i, no. 4 (Oct 1980), p. 287.

[2] *Modern Language Journal*, lviii, no. 7 (Nov 1976).

[3] _____ : p. 340.

excellent one — but the more serious peril is from language which disarms, but does not smell as it does so, so that one suffers its effects without being aware of its presence.

Mr I.D. Hill, who works for the Medical Research Council as a statistician, also has views on 'complex'. In a very helpful and detailed letter,[4] he takes me to task, quite rightly, for failing to make a distinction between words which can well be diseased as used by non-specialists, but precise and useful terms in the hands of the specialists themselves. 'Construct' and 'dimension' are examples of what he has in mind, and so is 'complex', but the situation here, he believes, is more complicated and perhaps more sinister. 'The psychologists, of course have no right', he says, 'to take a common English word, give it a technical meaning, and then say that it shall not be used except in their specialised sense. But the common English meaning is as an adjective. It is the use as a noun, by those who do not know what it means, that is diseased.'

This amounts to saying that the specialists' 'good' words have been so maltreated by amateurs that they are no longer of any use as technical terms. Mr Hill instances 'combinations' and 'permutations'. These, he says, are 'precise and useful mathematical terms that have been almost destroyed by misuse. Permutations is now in such widespread use to mean combinations, in football pools and elsewhere, that when Rubik's cube advertisements actually needed to talk about the number of permutations into which it can be put, the word would not do. So what word did they use instead — combinations!'

A similar disaster, as Mr Hill points out, is occurring to 'parameter'. 'I am,' he says, 'fighting a losing battle against the misuse of this word. It is being more and more used in medical and 'social science' papers simply to mean a variable or a feature. Its true uses in mathematics, statistics, and computer science are precise, useful and closely related to each other, but we are losing it and we may have to invent another word for the concept soon.' And so with 'statement' and 'infinite', both corrupted beyond recall by ignorant popularization and take-overs.

Mr Hill has two qualities in common with most of the people who have written to me. He has a good ear for the absurd and he feels that the merchants of disease will usually win in the end. One hopes he is wrong about the second, but for the first he has some pleasant illustrations, such as the BBC football commentator who said, 'the referee blows his whistle for the half-time situation', and the politician's 'We stand by our target'. 'Not really a sensible place to stand', as Mr Hill points out.

4   31 March 1982.

It is the people who collect examples of Diseased English from within the specialist field of their own work who are particularly helpful in getting together the evidence one needs, and I have been very fortunate in this respect. Lawyers, doctors, civil servants, teachers, economists and ministers of religion on both sides of the Atlantic have written to me with agreeable treachery about the linguistic crimes and fatuities of their colleagues.

Miss Dorothy Crocker, for example, has kept a close watch for many years on the nonsense produced at educational conferences, a very rich source indeed of Diseased English. She recalls a delegate to a conference of the National Union of Teachers (NUT) telling his willing listeners that 'Grammar schools are an obscenity and an obsolete obscenity',[5] and she has very kindly sent me from her files a vintage passage from the President's address at the National Association of Head Teachers Conference in the same year.[6]

After giving his opinion that comprehensive education had come into being in the UK not for political reasons, but as a result of 'man's instinct for survival', he noted with pleasure that most teachers had 'learned to adapt with dignity', but some, unfortunately, had 'resisted the call of reality' for much longer. He then continued: 'They manage to retain for some time an aura of non-conformist glamour which begins as the arrogance of the rugged individualist, slips sadly into the faded charm of a world only vaguely remembered, and finally declines into an object of pity enshrined for ever within the triple pillars of Black Papers and referred to only in moments of deep nostalgia by aspirants for (*sic*) ministerial office whose ambition has so far failed to appreciate that you cannot politically assassinate those who are politically dead'. 'Write down the meaning of that in one sentence,' as one could have said to a boy or girl in the days when précis-writing was still regarded as a useful exercise and not as 'obscene' or 'élitist'. And even a very bright pupil would have found the task far from easy.

The Dictionary of Diseased English, in its pursuit, knife in hand, of music, art and literary critics who appeared to have temporarily forgotten their duty to communicate, included an entry for Painter-liness. I had been unable to discover any definition of this in print and since my artistic friends appeared to be rather vague as to its meaning, I found myself forced to guess my way towards an interpretation. Three

---

[5]   Birmingham, Easter 1977.
[6]   June 1977.

years later[7] I received a friendly letter from Mr David Russell, who lives in Florence. He had, he said, recently bought the book, which had, by that time, reached the shops in Italy, and after praising it in the most generous terms, he came to the little matter of Painterliness and Painterly:

> 'As a painter and art critic myself, I have never heard the word used in the sense you give it, that is to say referring to the painter and not to his work. Painterly, in my experience, is always used to describe a certain type of painting, the kind of painting that exploits the medium of (generally) oil-painting to its maximum, that is to say impasto, glazes, 'fat and lean' qualities of the oil and pigment, and so on ... the sensual aspect of the use of the colours. So Unpainterly normally would be used to describe a kind of painting (constructivism, for example) where the paint is laid on without much regard for its richness or sensual effect. Somebody like Van Gogh would probably be the example of the 'painterly painter', one who exploits the medium to its maximum effect.'

Mr Russell's letter is a particularly agreeable example of the community of scholars, to which I referred earlier. It is also an indication that, like any other dictionary, a *Dictionary of Diseased English* can never be finished, which was the main reason for deciding to prepare and publish a successor, *The Dictionary of Even More Diseased English*. The title of this new book deliberately and economically has two meanings. It contains even more examples of Diseased English and many of its examples are even more diseased than those to be found in the original work, which is another way of saying that the situation has got worse rather than better.

I have been content to let the first book stand on its own. Its range of entries gave, I feel, a reasonably good idea of Diseased English as it was in the second half of the 1970s and, if it were being reprinted again, the only changes I should want to make would be the kind of corrections required to meet the points made by such well-informed observers of the linguistic scene as Mr Hill and Mr Russell. Its introductory chapter was, so to speak, my Credo and it would be a waste of precious space to repeat it here.

Both the first and the second book, however, may be considered by some to be dictionaries of a strange type. In defence of the name and the

[7]   8 Dec 1980.

form, I should like to say that only one duty is laid on the dictionary-maker; his entries must be arranged in alphabetical order, so that it can be consulted easily. Dictionaries have passed through many stages of development, beginning in the 16th century as explanations of 'hard words', moving on to being attempts to regularize spelling and to lay down standards of correct usage, and ending, early in the present century, as comprehensive lists of all the 'respectable' words to be found in printed sources, past and present. During the subsequent decades, there have been a number of separate dictionaries of non-respectable words, although these have never been complete, and more recently one or two trials have been made to blend the two approaches, that is, to cease putting words into categories and to combine first quality, second quality and third quality words into a single book.

Yet, whatever one's approach may be, there are limits to what any dictionary can achieve, even one as huge and as supplement-enriched as the great *New English Dictionary*. Some form of selection is unavoidable. If one's aim is to include all words, or even all 'good' words, the entries must necessarily be brief, and any assessment confined to such simple labels as 'obsolete', 'colloquial' and 'obscene'. A quite different method, which is the one I have adopted, is to use a dictionary to illustrate and discuss a particular theme. This seems to me to be perfectly reasonable, provided readers understand clearly what they are being offered. And what they are being offered by the present work and its predecessor, and by my *Dictionary of the Teenage Revolution and its Aftermath*, also published this year, is a collection of short and, in certain instances, perhaps provocative essays on particular words and phrases. The opinions and attitudes are my own and no doubt they will please and annoy people in much the same way as those reflected in *The Dictionary of Diseased English* and, in the process, produce the same generous crop of new information.

Two points should, perhaps, be made about the sources. The first is that the quotations given in the *Dictionary* do not necessarily reflect the views of the newspaper, magazine or broadcasting organization which published it. They may have come from an advertisement or from a letter to the paper. And the second point is that the large number of examples from particular publications, such as *The Daily Telegraph* and the *New Yorker*, does not imply that they are exceptionally likely to print Diseased English. All that can be deduced from this high degree of representation is that these are influential and widely read titles and that, for this reason, I have read them regularly and with particular care.

A

Account
A customer. At one time — it seems long, long ago, in the golden days of commercial innocence — an account was an impersonal affair, a set of figures, the bookkeeping entries relating to a firm or an individual. Recently, however, it has taken on human form, as a piece of mathematics on two legs, to be talked to, respected, persuaded and manipulated. It can be demanded of a firm's representatives that 'they will be experienced in negotiating with Key Accounts' (*Sunday Telegraph*, 15 Nov 1981). The use of the capital letters here increases the degree and feeling of personification.

Achievement oriented
With one's eyes permanently fixed on the attainment of profitable results. A firm, eager to impress the business world, will therefore advertise, not for a couple of experienced managers, but for 'two high-calibre achievement oriented managers' (*The Daily Telegraph*, 8 Feb 1982), which seems a little like emphasizing the obvious, since how many 'high-calibre' managers are not 'achievement oriented'? It is rather similar to asking for a good swimmer who must be able to swim well.

Action-orientated
Energetic. In the management jargon of today, 'oriented' and 'orientated' are interchangeable, so far as their meaning or non-meaning are concerned, although 'orientated' is slightly classier, because it has an extra syllable. Both, however, are nonsense words, which do nothing whatever to increase understanding. It is highly unlikely that anyone looking for a job will be much impressed by being offered 'the chance to join a team of action-orientated professionals in our London office' (*Sunday Telegraph*, 3 Jan 1982), although wordiness of this order undoubtedly makes the recruitment agency feel good and the newspaper with space to sell even better. One may be permitted, perhaps, to ask what the opposite of 'action-orientated' would be. Work-shy?

1

Bone-idle? One is struck by the awful possibility that not all 'professionals' are 'action-orientated'. This cannot be so. Perhaps some are more 'action-orientated' than others.

Adult

Pornographic, promiscuous, perverted. The word is a sick joke, a sad paradox in a minor key, since the one certain feature of pornography, promiscuity and perversion is that they are not adult. However, those for whom these human frailties spell profit and those who shy away from the blunt term think otherwise. 'Adult' is a well-liked cover-up term for much that is unpleasant and degrading — 'Unused adult photo sets' (*New Musical Express*, 18 July 1958), and 'Black man, 76, looking for women, 18-60, for adult games' (*Screw West*, 6 June 1979) make the point. The euphemism continues to be as popular as ever, and in present circumstances one can do little more than pray for its decease.

Amenities

Interesting, agreeable features. But what is one to make of 'a town well served by amenities' (*The Daily Telegraph*, 17 Sept 1981)? 'Well served by buses' or 'well served by the police' one can understand, since buses and policemen are active, they do something, but how can a town be 'served' by its parks, its roadside trees or the other pieces of pleasantness which make a place more liveable and tolerable? There must always be some argument as to what does and does not constitute an amenity. A dog would no doubt consider a lamppost an amenity, but its master would be more likely to classify it as a public utility. An 'amenity' is not the same as a utility or a resource, although the nation's house agents tend to lump everything in together, so that schools, bingo halls, hairdressers and Chinese take-aways are all brought under the same heading of 'amenity'. Houses, curiously enough, are not 'amenities'. They do, however, contain 'amenities'.

Aggressive

Persistent, eager to clinch a deal, win business. This unpleasant word and the qualities associated with it go from strength to strength in the modern business world, where elbows are considered one of the most important parts of the anatomy and where the world is a perpetual, glorious battlefield. Research people and secretaries are not usually required to be aggressive, but for a member of the sales force, aggressiveness is assumed. A firm will therefore announce, 'We require an aggressive chemical salesperson' (*Sunday Telegraph*, 2 Dec 1981) almost as if 'aggressive salesperson' were a compound noun. And, businessmen being the super-serious creatures they are, the thought that there might be irreverent people who would find the idea of 'an aggressive chemical salesperson' rather funny never arises.

But, the brutal world of industry and commerce apart, one is surely entitled to have misgivings about the idea of an aggressive doctor. The Americans, however, appear to have no such worries, since a New York clinic can advertise 'a challenging position for an aggressive, creative and open-minded individual' (*New York Times*, 17 Sept 1981). One hopes that his aggressiveness is confined to selling the facilities offered by the clinic and that no part of it spills over into the treatment and handling of patients.

Yet, awful as the prospect of being cared for by an aggressive doctor may be, it is as nothing compared with the threat of being hit by an aggressive target. For those who may not have thought of this terrifying possibility, one must issue a warning that, in one firm at least, 'aggressive targets are being set for sales growth based on positive marketing' (*The Daily Telegraph*, 23 Dec 1981).

Ample

Until recently, 'ample' was a polite term for 'big' or 'plenty'. Ladies had ample bosoms, restaurants served ample meals and one arrived in ample time for one's appointment. The euphemism was well understood and caused little trouble. In the hands of today's estate agents, however, 'ample' can hardly be said to make for easy or accurate communication. A house is advertised as offering 'ample garaging (5/6 cars)' (*Country Life*, 21 May 1981) is in the old ample bosom tradition. The house simply has a very big garage, but it would be vulgar to say so. What, however, is implied in this description of a desirable property in Devon? 'Apart from its eight bedrooms, four bathrooms and four reception rooms, it has ample frontage to the River Dart' (*The Times*, 12 Aug 1981). Ample for what? For mooring a small motorboat, a warship or a car ferry? What is probably meant is that the house has a large enough river frontage to make one's friends and acquaintances envious, long enough to convince the world that its owner must have a great deal of money, long enough to be a suitable companion to eight bedrooms, four bathrooms and four reception rooms, long enough to maintain one's social position at its appropriate level.

But what is ample for one person may be more or less than ample for another. There is no scientifically agreed standard of ampleness. Consider the house in New England which has, one is told, 'ample closet space' (*Boston Globe*, 11 Oct 1981). Ample for whom? For a family of six? For an old lady living on her own? For every conceivable occupant? Such infinitely elastic cupboard space has, alas, never yet existed.

And much more

Plus one or two other things. This is one of today's major confidence tricks. One can blow it wide open simply by asking how much more, but few people do, because there is usually no-one available to answer the question, no-one to shoot. So Delta Airlines can announce 'In-flight entertainment. Superb cuisine. Fine wines and liqueurs. And much more.' (*The Daily Telegraph*, 15 June 1982), in the knowledge that only the very rare person will attempt to call their bluff by requesting a list of all these imaginary extras.

And the Old Ship Hotel, Brighton, can make the same assumption about its advertisement for all-inclusive weekends. Among the attractions offered here are '*Activities*. At Hotel: Games room, bridge, free bike hire. Outside (at specially arranged prices): Golf, squash, riding, sea fishing and much more' (advertisement in *The Daily Telegraph*, 19 Jan 1983). Now what could these other outdoor activities be, one wonders? Walking, perhaps? Or kite-flying? Organized leapfrog? Are there really so many that they cannot be listed? Or so secret that they cannot be published?

Answer to

Is responsible to. For reasons which one can only guess at, modern management seems to dislike the idea of one person being responsible to another and prefers such military-sounding, line-of-command phrases as 'report to' and 'answer to'. Sometimes, however, language goes a little astray, with some confusion between the job and the person who holds it. We then get such splendidly nonsensical phrases as 'The post answers directly to the Managing Director' (*The Sunday Times*, 25 Oct 1981), which brings the age of robots terrifyingly close.

Antiqued

Finished in such a way as to make something look much older than it really is. This word was included in *The Dictionary of Diseased English*, with the comment that it had become common in the USA and so 'can hardly fail to cross the Atlantic in time'. Fortunately, that sad day has not yet arrived and it is still, for some strange reason, an all-American word. The lucky inhabitants of Omaha and Dallas, unlike those of Portsmouth and Bradford, can become the proud owners of 'crystal framed in antiqued brass' (*New York Times*, 27 Sept 1981).

Arms length

Getting one's hands dirty, possessing practical skill and being ready to use it. In the industrial/commercial world, this trendy expression signifies, heaven knows why, precisely the opposite of what might be expected, given that 'to hold someone at arm's length' means 'to keep someone at a distance'. The new, perverse use is illustrated by 'A sound technical knowledge of lubricants coupled with an ability to operate on an arms length basis is an essential part of the job' (*The Daily Telegraph*, 19 Feb 1982). Since the apostrophe is rarely inserted, it is impossible to know whether one arm is involved or two.

Articulate (i)

Able to speak. This has become a great favourite with those engaged in the business of industrial recruitment at the higher levels. Owing no doubt to some bad experiences in the recent past, it is now apparently considered necessary to specify that prospective managers shall be capable of intelligible speech. It is now entirely normal for a firm to announce that it wishes to appoint 'a number of highly motivated and articulate young mechanical engineers' (*Edinburgh Evening News*, 6 Nov 1981). Whether the inclusion of 'highly motivated and articulate' in the advertisement makes the slightest difference to the application list is, of course, a matter of opinion.

Articulate (ii)

To put into words. 'This with-it word has so far been confined to America' decided *The Dictionary of Diseased English* in 1977, and it is a pleasure to be able to report that this is still the case, except in certain academic circles, where the use of plain language is a serious bar to promotion. But in the USA to 'articulate', instead of to 'express' or 'publish', is solid evidence of good breeding and scholarly worth — 'Although articulated 20 years ago, it is difficult to say how often or successfully this approach has been implemented' (*British Psychological Bulletin*, xc (1981), no.2).

Assertive

Well publicized, strong, impossible to overlook. *The Dictionary of Diseased English* drew attention to the popularity of this term with wine writers, a fashion which has fortunately passed, although its usage still crops up from time to time among those lesser members of the tribe who find themselves temporarily at a loss for words to describe a particularly ecstatic tingling of the taste-buds. But commercial and industrial people, alas, grow steadily more fond of it, and it is now possible even for an institution as restrained and respectable as a bank to refer to 'our policy of assertive growth' (*New Yorker*, 28 Sept 1981).

Augment

Increase, enlarge. The battle against this piece of management pomposity is probably lost, although one has a duty to go on fighting. Just why 'augment' is reckoned to confer superior status on the people using it is not at all clear, except that it is a word nobody uses in conversation and therefore, by a perverted logic, especially desirable among the semi-literate, who are, most unfortunately, thick on the ground in the world of industry and commerce in both the UK and the USA, people who feel that the enterprise they control is graded up by such sentences as 'They now wish to augment their team working on new materials and processes' (*The Daily Telegraph*, 10 Dec 1981).

Award-winning

Exceptionally good, fashionable, desirable. The scale and effrontery of this confidence trick gets worse with every year that passes. The trick is never under any circumstances to specify what the award was and who made it. 'Award-winning' belongs to the 'oilier oil', 'washes whiter' category of advertising swindle, in which no decent member of the public is supposed to ask 'oilier than what?', 'whiter than what?' There are now welcome signs, however, that 'award-winning' may be exhausting itself through absurd over-use. It is still, however, much with us at the moment, although quite how effective it is as a selling tool nowadays, in its old age, is difficult to decide. Does it really add much vigour and magic to such masterpieces of selling copy as '17 acres of award-winning grounds to stroll over' (*Boston Globe*, 11 Oct 1981), or 'Central location, award-winning design' (*New York Times*, 27 Sept 1981), or 'Our client's success with Award Winning world acclaimed technology' (*The Daily Telegraph*, 8 June 1982), or 'Award-winning editorial environment' (*New Yorker*, 7 June 1982)?

Aware

Sharp, wide-awake. At one time, one had to be aware of something. Now it is sufficient to be simply 'aware', with the context supplied by the advantage of belonging to the same cultural group as the person who is 'aware'. So, in the case of 'candidates should be mature, experienced and aware businessmen' (*The Sunday Times*, 25 Oct 1981), the public at large may well be puzzled by 'aware', but businessmen themselves will know what kind of awareness is expected of them, they will understand the code and react accordingly. They will realize that an 'aware' sales manager or a financial controller is quite different from an 'aware' member of the drug-culture, but they will also be flattered and toned-up by having such a modern adjective applied to them. To be 'sharp' or 'wide-awake' would be to have oneself described as a very old-fashioned businessman indeed. 'Aware' is a great help in concealing some of the more unpleasant aspects of commercial practice.

But the absurdities of 'aware' are not confined to the business world. On the contrary, businessmen did no more than take over a well-established hippy word, which is still in vogue and thriving among members of the radical and caring Left, who are capable of writing and speaking such verbose nonsense as 'the recent and welcome evolution of the Scout movement into a more socially aware and relevant organisation' (*The Daily Telegraph*, 2 Dec 1982). *The Daily Telegraph*, one should in fairness point out, was not personally responsible for this rubbish. It was merely carrying out its duty in quoting the Chairman of the Further and Higher Education Committee of the Inner London Education Authority, a body obsessed these days with the need to be aware and relevant, that is, unmistakably socialist, in all it does.

B

Background
Experience. As used by what is flatteringly called industry, this word has become both a plague and an absurdity. Until the 1950s, a person's 'background' was his family and education, the dual foundation on which his life was built. From then on, 'background' increasingly came to mean, within business circles, one's working experience and field of specialization, the implication being that the job was the man, and that nothing else mattered. Since the industrial world is not celebrated for its sense of humour, such mirth-provoking sentences as the following became not only possible but normal — 'You will have a petroleum background' (*The Daily Telegraph*, 21 Jan 1982) and, even more splendid, 'Your background will be crusty bread' (*Edinburgh Evening News*, 6 Nov 1981). A piece of cheese may very suitably have a background of crusty bread, but surely not a human being?

Basic cleansing bar
A piece of soap. The wheel of fashion has gone full circle. After years of successfully persuading women with more money than sense that the way to everlasting youth and beauty was through expensive preparations in pots and tubes and even more expensive applications of mud and steam, administered by people with diplomas in mud and steam, soap came to seem not only old-fashioned but positively dangerous, the enemy of the skin. It also had the serious disadvantage of being cheap. Once it had retreated sufficiently far into the past, however, the road was clear to reintroduce it as a precious and costly novelty, a profitable innovation which has now taken place — 'Basic cleansing bar for dry or oily skins, £6.00' (*The Times*, 5 Jan 1982).

Best
Highest, most. Weather forecasts are no place for value judgements. A temperature of 20°C is not 'better' than one of 5°, a rainy day is not 'worse' than a sunny day. This fact was generally acknowledged within the

meteorology business, until the broadcasting authorities began to see the possibilities of weather forecasting as a public relations tool. Since the urban and suburban population of the UK, the great bulk of listeners and viewers, prefer sunshine to rain and would, if they had the ordering of such matters, opt for perpetual and unbroken blue skies, the way to their hearts was clearly to write the weather forecasts along the same lines, abandoning all pretensions to scientific objectivity and giving the customers what they want to hear. So a new breed of popular entertainers was created, dressed like weather forecasters and assuring the public, ever-eager for good news, that 'the best of the sunshine will be in the North-East' (BBC Radio 4, 7.55 am, 10 June 1982), and that 'the best temperatures will be in the North of England' (BBC Radio 4, 12.55 pm, 31 July 1982).

Big
Fat. Tall people in search of clothes to fit them do well to avoid anything which suggests that it is intended for someone 'big', a word which always indicates girth and bulk, not height. Just occasionally the retailer takes trouble to make this clear, as in 'South's largest specialty store for big and tall men' (*Your Houston Shopping Guide*, Greater Houston Convention and Visitors Council, 1982).

Bill, etcetera
William, etcetera. The use of shortened Christian names is yet another first-line confidence trick, designed to show that the person referred to is a democrat to his fingertips, the friend of all, always approachable and without an ounce of superiority in his make-up. It is false and a fraud, because it implies a close relationship which does not in fact exist. When the practice occurs among people of some eminence, it is doubly despicable, partly because it suggests a degree of intimacy which cannot be true and partly because such deliberate slumming is an affront to dignity. 'We welcome to the studio the Bishop of Edmonton, Bill Westwood' (BBC *Today* programme, 4 Dec 1981) does neither the speaker nor the Bishop any credit. The habit could very fairly be called the Tony Benn swindle.

Breathtaking
Better than average. A favourite word among novel-reviewers on both sides of the Atlantic, a ridiculous race of unhelpful time-servers who, by perpetually searching for language with which to pretend that the mediocre is brilliant, have made it impossible to take many a good word

seriously any longer. 'Breathtaking — an extraordinary blend of bitter self-denigration and sweet recollection', writes one of these literary parasites of an American novel (*New Yorker*, 20 Sept 1982), as if the novel were the equivalent of Scottish mountains on an autumn morning. Each year they will have no difficulty in discovering a dozen such novels, which shows how easily some people's breath is taken.

Blue-chip
Sound, reliable. This expression is getting out of hand. One knew where one was with blue-chip shares and, up to a point, with blue-chip companies, although in the case of the companies the term has often been recklessly used, so that 'a blue-chip company' can mean nothing more than a big company, and size, as we well know, is no guarantee of soundness. Consequently, to say of someone that he is 'currently with a blue-chip company' (*The Daily Telegraph*, 10 Dec 1981) may mean a great deal or very little, and 'a graduate with previous blue-chip experience of holding broad administrative management responsibilities' (*The Daily Telegraph*, 10 Dec 1981) is an examination piece for advanced students of contemporary English. Is the graduate supposed to have obtained this experience with blue-chip companies, or is it the experience itself which is blue-chip? If the second interpretation is correct, then one may be forced to think again about what 'blue-chip' means, since it is possible to gain very valuable, that is, 'blue-chip' experience, by working for a while with an extremely bad organization, a fact of which many extremely able accountants are well aware. The assumption that blue-chip experience is to be had only with a blue-chip company is certainly untrue. The safest plan is probably to avoid the expression altogether, since there is no longer any common agreement as to what it really does mean.

Broadgauged
With wide interests, able to turn a capable hand to a variety of tasks. The business world has become very fond of this word and one can easily understand why. Because of the railway analogy, it suggests stability, solidity and comfort, yet at the same time it is conveniently vague. Few people are likely to resent being called broadgauged — to be accused of being narrowgauged would certainly be considered offensive — but equally few would be able to describe the qualities with which they were being credited. One would be pleased and flattered to reply to an advertisement demanding 'an extremely competent broadgauged individual' (*Boston Globe*, 11 Oct 1981).

Budget

Low, affordable. In our mealymouthed, snobbish society, nothing can ever be advertised as 'cheap', a good, simple word which decades of commercial malpractice has made synonymous with 'nasty'. 'Inexpensive', however, is perfectly in order, and, in their frantic and never-ending search for equally harmless alternatives, those with goods and services to sell have come up with 'budget' — 'First-class holidays, budget prices' (*Sunday Telegraph*, 3 Jan 1982) — a word which is the answer to many commercial prayers.

'Budget' should, however, be approached with caution, since one person's budget is not necessarily another's. What would fit comfortably into the personal budget of a Saudi oil sheikh would bankrupt a car worker in Birmingham. 'Budget' is a very loose and relative term but, because of its vagueness, it does excellently as bait on the advertiser's hook. *See also* ECONOMICAL.

C

Capability

Ability. A great many of the world's people may have the capability to play the piano well or to speak Serbo-Croat fluently, but, for one reason or another, few have the ability to do so. The distinction between the two does not always appear to be well understood, so that serious misunderstandings are possible. How, for example, is one to interpret, 'Linguistic capability preferable' (*The Daily Telegraph*, 18 Feb 1982)? Is the candidate for the post expected to be already in possession of a good knowledge of Arabic, or whatever, or is it merely necessary that he should have the kind of mind which would allow him to learn the language quickly? The first implies capability, the second ability, and one can well imagine that, whichever was intended, a number of applicants would be wasting their time.

The great 18th-century landscape gardener, Lancelot 'Capability' Brown, obtained his nickname, not as a tribute to his ability, which was considerable, but from his somewhat tedious habit of saying, when visiting the estate of a prospective client, 'I see great capability of improvement here.' No reasonably well educated person in the 18th century would have confused the two, but few people today have the respect for precise language which the age of 'Capability' Brown took for granted.

Capitals, use of

In 18th-century Britain and America, it was still common to write and print nouns with an initial capital. The Germans, of course, still do, but the habit has died out in the Anglo-Saxon countries, except in certain not fully literate sections of the business world, where the use of capitals is reckoned to make words appear more important. The belief is mistaken, because all that is in fact achieved is an indulgent smile at a bizarre habit. To refer to 'a leading firm of Architects with a large U.K. and International Practice' (*The Sunday Times*, 25 Oct 1981) is to cause the reader to wonder where and how the person responsible for such oddities was brought up, which cannot surely have been the original intention.

Caring

Sentimental, publicly warm-hearted. This has become a tedious and much-used word, especially popular among readers of *The Guardian* and *New Society*, both of which publications are liable to refer at any moment to such concepts as 'the caring professions', 'the caring society', and 'a caring person'. One is not required to care for anything or anyone in particular. One just cares, a state of mind which not infrequently involves an impertinent degree of intrusion in other people's lives.

The word is so loosely used that it often means absolutely nothing at all. What, for instance, can a novel reviewer possibly have in mind when she writes of 'this caring, exquisitely wrought book' (*New Yorker*, 20 Sept 1981)? If, for 'caring', we were to substitute 'nosey parkerish', we should probably not be very wide of the mark.

Challenging

Difficult, badly in need of improvement, full of dreadful and probably unsolvable problems. Those seeking new employment should beware of advertisements containing the word 'challenging'. It nearly always means that the job in question will subject its holder to intolerable strains and frustrations and that only a person of exceptional stamina is likely to survive and prosper. So, prospective sales managers for gas turbines should, at interview, ask some particularly searching questions, when they are told that 'this challenging position calls for a highly motivated person' (*The Daily Telegraph*, 6 Jan 1982), and nothing but exhaustion and marital break-up faces those who are foolish enough to sell themselves body and soul to 'a fast moving, highly challenging environment' (*The Daily Telegraph*, 5 Nov 1981).

Char

Charcoal. In the UK one grills, in the USA one broils. In the UK food is charcoal grilled, in the USA, it is char broiled, and if one were to ask 100 British people what 'char broiled' meant, 97 of them would have no idea, additional confusion being caused by the fact that in the UK a 'char' was a charwoman, until the new classless society found it desirable and socially just to call her a cleaning lady.

Consequently, for a London hotel to offer on its menu 'Beefburgers, char broiled to your preference' (Park Lane Hotel, London, July 1982) is unlikely to make for quick comprehension or reliable ordering among its British customers, although visiting Americans would no doubt feel immediately at home. To use 'char broiled' in the UK is a piece of restaurant silliness, sheer mid-Atlantic snobbery, for which nobody is likely to feel particularly grateful.

Character

Individuality, style. As an estate agents' word, 'character' has been with us for many years, but certain recent developments, both in society and in the private world inhabited by estate agents, suggest that a reassessment of its meaning and of its power to impress, confuse and delude might not be out of place.

In the UK, as everywhere else in the Western world, 99 per cent of the population now live in accommodation which is neither distinctive nor distinguished. Every house is like tens of thousands of others. It has no personality of its own, nothing which would inspire its occupants to say that the place in which they lived was unique. The remaining one per cent, however, possess houses which are one-offs. Many of them, it is true, will bear a close resemblance to other one-offs but, above a certain price level, the complete photocopy is a rarity. This one per cent constitutes the nation's stock of Houses of Character. They are the houses which make an estate agent's life worthwhile and stimulate his finest prose. But, and it has to be said with all possible clarity and firmness, by no means all Houses of Character are elegant, appealing and lovable. Some of them are downright hideous, so dreadful in fact that, as a prospective purchaser, one yearns for a compulsory subdivision of Houses of Character into Houses of Good Character and Houses of Bad Character. That welcome development seems to be a long way off, however, and for the moment we have to learn to protect ourselves by holding the estate agents' descriptions up to the light, in order to see what lies hidden behind them. We have to train ourselves to distinguish between 'a family house of immense character' (*Country Life*, 21 May 1981), 'an exceptionally attractive character house' (*Country Life*, 21 Sept 1981), and 'a fine country house of great character' (*Country Life*, 21 May 1981), and to do that effectively demands a fine and cynical eye, long experience and a connoisseur's knowledge of the ways and thought patterns of estate agents.

Characterful

Full of character, in the estate agents' sense of that word. A 'characterful house' is one not to be confused with hundreds and thousands of others, a one-off. A slight complication is introduced when 'characterful' is used with a plural noun, as in 'The characterful villas are reminiscent of an Andalusian village' (Wings brochure, *Faraway Holidays*, Summer 1983). These holiday houses are, as the photograph makes clear, pleasant little places, not detached, but built in terraced groups. They have obviously received the attentions of an architect, whose skill has made the project worth looking at and, one hopes, worth living in. These particular examples are 'characterful' because they have charm and style, but others, graced with the same adjective, could be merely bizarre. To be 'characterful' is not enough. It all depends on the 'character'. *See also* VILLA.

Coated
Accompanied by. This new restaurant-word, born in the USA in the mid-1970s, reached London recently and will, no doubt, make its way to Birmingham, Newcastle and other gastronomic paradises in due course. For anyone who cares about food in the slightest it is likely to cause the appetite to disappear very fast indeed, implying as it does a great, thick, woollen blanket of sauce, totally masking the dish underneath. The association of 'coated' with painters and decorators is equally unstimulating to most discriminating eaters, although, among those who suffer badly from menu hypnosis, 'coated', and the thicker the better, may quite possibly suggest value for money. But anyway, here it is in our midst, a piece of fish 'coated with a Dutch sauce' (menu, Park Lane Hotel, London, July 1982). For those unfamiliar with the People's Democracy of restaurant translations, one should perhaps mention that 'a Dutch sauce' is intended to be the equivalent of *sauce hollandaise*, which has rather different overtones.

Cold larder, from the
Cold. Until the Restaurant Revolution, when poetry and circumlocution took over from plain statements, the customer was offered cold meat or, in slightly classier places, cold meats or cold buffet. These old-fashioned terms fortunately still exist but, in certain of the trendier places, where the milieu is considered more important than the food, one notices that dishes are no longer cold, but 'from the cold larder', which almost certainly means 'from the refrigerator', since few restaurants boast a larder these days. And so it is at the Great Northern Hotel, King's Cross, London, capitals and all — 'From the Cold Larder' (menu, July 1982). *See also* CAPITALS, USE OF.

Country-style

Rough, unsophisticated, peasant-like. 'Country-style pâté, with hot toast' (menu, Great Northern Hotel, King's Cross, London, July 1982) should indicate that the pâté is rather coarse-cut and is of a type which one might reasonably expect to find in a farmhouse in France. One cannot, alas, depend on this. When applied either to food or to music, 'country-style' may mean anything or nothing. The commercial intentions are all too obvious. In an urban society, to attach the label 'country' to cheese, butter, pâté or any other kind of food suggests, often quite wrongly, freshness, flavour, honest worth, traditional preparation and taste. It is probably safer to translate 'country-style pâté with hot toast' as 'pâté with hot toast'. Disappointment is less likely this way.

Committed to

Believing in, in favour of, interested in. The phrase has become extremely popular in academic and business circles, mainly, no doubt, because of its traditional moral and religious associations. Nowadays, one can 'commit' oneself or 'be committed' to the most trivial and materialistic activities, but contrive to elevate them to an altogether higher level, simply by using this extremely convenient expression. A firm making electronic equipment will therefore say that it is 'firmly committed to the concept of office automation' (*The Daily Telegraph*, 29 Jan 1982), while a medical journal is 'committed to research carried out within the increasingly broad conceptual framework to which the term 'psychosomatic' is applicable (advertisement card, Baywood Publishing Company, New York, Sept 1981).

One should, however, note that, in today's strange world, it is not necessary to be committed to anything in particular. One just has to be committed, a member of 'a vital, caring, committed community' (*New York Times*, 27 Sept 1981).

Commitment

Involvement, undertaking, course of action, policy. *See* COMMIT-TED.There is absolutely nothing wrong *per se* in committing oneself to a particular course of action or, having made a decision, to stick to it. What is both unpleasant and misleading, is to use words such as 'committed' and 'commitment', which traditionally have strong implications of moral duty, for activities which deserve a more neutral approach. To have a 'commitment' to feed, clothe and educate one's children is reasonable and good, to have a 'commitment' to burglary or wife beating is much less acceptable. The situation is, of course, bedevilled by the use of 'commitment' in the plural. One is accustomed to talk loosely, and often rather grandly, about one's 'commitments', or to say that one is 'heavily committed', ignoring the fact that some commitments are ennobling and others degrading.

'Commitment' today is yet another instance of searching continuously for words with which to give added tone and worth to one's business dealings. It is one of industry's list of sanctifying words. So an electronic power company will speak of 'our strong nuclear commitment' (*Boston Globe*, 11 Oct 1981), and an electronics firm will announce that 'to support this commitment, we have set up a systems and special products group' (*The Daily Telegraph*, 19 Jan 1982), the 'commitment' in this case being to 'the concept of automation', that is, 'to office automation', 'concept' being just another piece of impressive sounding verbosity, and totally redundant.

Worst of all, is the view that people need not have a 'commitment' to anything in particular. All that is required of them, as model employees and good citizens, is that they shall display something called 'commitment', which presumably means 'taking a keen interest in what they are doing' — 'Candidates should have a highly developed sense of commitment' (*The Daily Telegraph*, 10 Dec 1981) — and that, at a time when so many people appear to be interested in nothing at all, is certainly something.

Common law wife/husband

A person to whom one is not married, but with whom one lives as if one were. These marriages, established only be cohabitation and by the passage of time, have no standing in English law and the parties consequently have no marital rights or privileges, at least so far as the law is concerned. The persistent and increasing use of the terms 'common-law wife' and 'common-law husband', presumably for reasons of respectability, unfortunately encourages many people south of the Border — things are different in Scotland — to believe they have rights which do not in fact exist, a sad case of faulty language producing faulty ideas. However, the 'woman who turned her common-law husband into a human torch' (*The Daily Telegraph*, 20 Feb 1982), would probably have adopted the same tactics had she been married to him. There is nothing about common-law husbands which makes them particularly inflammable or indeed particularly deserving of such a fate.

Journalists, by the way, have become extremely fond of the phrase 'common-law wife', although rather less so of 'common-law husband'.

They are largely responsible for the spread of the term and therefore for its consequences.

Communication
Explanation, persuasion. 'Communication' has surely become one of the most absurd, brainwashing words in the English language. If one were to believe the experts and would-be experts, everyone has a communication problem these days. Sadly, they always did. To be misunderstood is a condition of being alive. The only person one understands is oneself, and then not always very well. But, just as the belief exists that there are short-cuts to health and that, if only there were more doctors and better doctors, more 'health-care', everybody could be perpetually 18, so there has developed a highly profitable industry to teach the virtues of 'communication' and to sell recipes for 'communication', conveniently ignoring the fact that getting one's ideas across to other people is, always has been and always will be very hard work, with only a limited chance of success.

Sentences like 'Communication skills, both oral and written, are of paramount importance' (*The Daily Telegraph*, 11 Dec 1981) obscure the nature and realities of the problem. 'Communication' is not a mechanical affair, nor are its 'skills' to be acquired through going on courses or receiving diplomas. One cannot communicate with people who do not want to be communicated with. 'Communication' between Protestants and Catholics in Ulster, or between the Conservative Party and the extreme Left, or between devout Christians and atheists, is stillborn. It cannot grow, because the emotional barriers are too great. The language of understanding is not there, and 'communication skills' are irrelevant to the situation. To professionalize 'communication' is nearly always to trivialize it. Whenever one comes up against the word 'communication' nowadays, one should never take it at its face value, despite all the commercial pressures to do so. One should ask, "In its context, what exactly does the word mean? What kind of 'communication' is the author talking about? What level or intensity of understanding is envisaged?" These are rarely popular questions because so many people earn such a good living from 'communication'.

Community publisher
Publisher of books based on the reminiscences of people living in the area. This is not a term to which one can extend a wholehearted welcome, mainly because most people would give it every meaning but the correct one. Some could certainly think it meant 'a publisher

operating his business within the community and for the financial benefit of the community', but this is only rarely the case. Few 'community publishers' expect to make much, if any, money out of the venture. They are usually motivated by the praiseworthy wish to give ordinary people a chance to give their version of history and of the modest, but usually neglected part which they played in it. There is no quarrel whatever with the activity of the 'community publishers'. The criticism is of the peculiar and misleading name they have bestowed on themselves, united as they are into a 'Federation of worker writers and community publishers' (*List of Member Groups*, 1980). *See also* WORKER WRITERS.

Compact
Small, but not too small. Nothing in business is ever small. It can decently be 'a limited number', 'fast-growing', 'young' or 'compact', but never small, because, in the business world, small is not beautiful at all. It suggests failure, vulnerability. 'Compact' is an excellent word in every way, giving the impression that an organization is without waste or fat, that its correct size has been calculated to a nicety, and that every part of it is bound tightly and efficiently to the rest. But the clients who are 'reinforcing their compact marketing orientated management team' (*The Sunday Times*, 25 Oct 1981) still have nothing more or less than a small management team.

Compensation
The reward for one's labours. The word, although very widely used, is fundamentally wrong. One can properly receive 'compensation' only in exchange for something unpleasant, such as an injury or an accident. The Workmen's Compensation Act was constructed around precisely this interpretation. If, however, one is referring to what is given in payment for toil, the implication must be that the toil in question is in some way unpleasant. This may well be so, but it would seem wise not to advertise the fact in advance, as a great many firms now do, announcing, for instance, that 'both positions carry an excellent compensation and benefits package' (*The Daily Telegraph*, 18 Dec 1981). In this particular case, since 'benefits' are mentioned in addition to 'compensation', it is difficult to see what 'compensation' can be, apart from salary. One cannot very well imagine any of the usual managerial perks which is not a benefit. It could be, however, that modern business has now become so refined and gentlemanly that 'salary', and even 'remuneration' are coarse, rude words.

Complimentary
Free. An old chestnut, but more and more people are taken in by it each year, so there seems to be no harm in turning another spotlight on it. In business, nothing is ever free. Someone has to pay for it and it could be you, in your innocence. 'Complimentary' makes the truth much easier to conceal, and, in any case, 'free' is commercially obscene.

When Western Airlines tells its passengers, or some of them, 'We'll fly you in comfort to Phoenix, Arizona, while you sit sipping complimentary champagne' (*The Times*, 5 Dec 1981), they are offering a rather skilfully laundered version of the facts. The champagne is free only in the sense that the person drinking it has made no direct and conscious payment for it. But some part of the profit of his and every other passenger's flight has necessarily gone towards the free champagne fund. The champagne is not free, but it feels free. So too does the package holiday bonus so temptingly dangled before the faces of prospective adult patrons in the form of 'our complimentary "Just the Kids" program' (*Boston Globe*, 11 Oct 1981). No-one asks the tour operator, 'Who's paying for that, then?' Such a question would indeed be ingratitude of the worst sort, biting the holiday hand that feeds you. Such is the magic of 'complimentary'.

Coney
Rabbit. An ancient confidence trick which refuses to die, mainly because there is a never-ending supply of silly women who want to believe it. Each generation falls all over again for 'Made in real soft rich coney fur' (*Sunday Telegraph*, 8 Nov 1981), in a way they never would for 'real soft rich rabbit fur'. Yet, once one breaks the taboo, rabbit fur seems much warmer, cosier and more cuddly than coney fur which, to one person at least, has a rather rat-like sound about it.

Contemporary modern
Contemporary. Those whose business is concerned with selling houses and furniture have always found themselves in adjectival difficulties of one kind and another. There have been particular headaches in distinguishing 'in a saleable way' between the various styles produced by designers and architects who, during the present century, have turned their back on tradition, often with bizarre results. The dividing line between 'modern', 'ultra-modern' and 'contemporary' has not invariably been easy for the layman to comprehend and one has a nasty suspicion that he is being discouraged from asking for precise definitions. In recent years, the Americans have made the fog of confusion

even thicker by inventing something called 'contemporary modern', with firms offering a full range of 'styles from contemporary modern to traditional' (*New York Times*, 27 Sept 1981). Until one is presented with 'contemporary ultra-modern', the situation can get no crazier. *See also* ULTRA-CONTEMPORARY.

Copiously
Well, thoroughly. Or so one has to suppose. This is now a much-liked novel-reviewers' word on both sides of the Atlantic. It is nearly always found in combination with 'researched' — 'Fascinating, copiously researched' (*New York Review of Books*, 3 Dec 1981). One could perhaps be pardoned for not considering it the happiest of terms, since it suggests only quantity, leaving the quality and effectiveness of the research to one's imagination and generosity. Had the book been 'thoroughly researched', one would have been inclined to think better of it. As it is, one is left with the strong suspicion that the reviewer makes no distinction between quality and quantity, a thought which is borne out by many of the novels published each year.

Corporate identity
A firm's image, the means by which such an image is created and developed. The problem of corporate identity only arises when a company has a complex structure, often as a result of mergers, so that customers and the general public are unaware, or insufficiently aware, that all the bits belong together. Considerable pains may then be taken, if this suits the company's interests, to emphasize the group's common identity by such means as portmanteau-type notepaper headings, symbols and a uniform style of advertising and report publication. But these devices are not in themselves the firm's corporate identity. They are merely its servants and agents, a fact which is frequently forgotten by those who are in the habit of confusing the letter and the spirit. 'Gough Brothers is currently redesigning its corporate identity' (*The Daily Telegraph*, 29 Jan 1982) is a typical example of this perverted modern habit of pretending the cart is the horse, or, even worse, of failing to understand the difference between the two.

Craft
To make, manufacture. This fashionable, nauseating and unnecessary verb entered the UK from the USA through the advertising back door. Its history is briefly as follows. When the stage had been reached where practically everything one bought was machine-made and mass-

produced, anything even partly made by hand had great rarity value and could command a luxury price. It did not have to be beautiful, well-made or well-designed. The fact that someone had worked on it with hand tools was sufficient to place it on a pedestal, and words like 'craftsman', 'craftsmanship' and 'crafts' were spoken in a tone of reverence and with half-closed eyes. From there it was only a short step to an appropriately exalted verb, and 'craft' duly appeared, in such sentences as 'Since it will take time to craft these beautiful porcelain miniatures ...' (*Sunday Telegraph*, 11 Aug 1982).

But let no-one be deceived. To make the master did indeed take the artist quite a long time, and one hopes she or he was paid a suitable fee. Once that was done, however, 'these beautiful porcelain miniatures' could be turned out in any required quantity and at fair speed. The original design and the mould were craftsmen's work and in that sense 'crafted', if one must use the word; the miniatures, the objects one actually received, were simply manufactured and, of course, none the worse for that.

Creativity

Life, liveliness. 'Creativity' is the ability to create things or ideas, or the activity which achieves such a result. To turn it into a synonym for 'bustle', 'excitement', or 'lots going on', is to mislead the reader and to rob the language of a useful and necessary word. But the American advertisers are doing precisely this, and their British rivals and admirers will, no doubt, soon be doing the same. An American advertisement for holidays in Mexico assures those teetering on the edge of parting with their dollars for such a purpose that, once in Mexico, they will find 'marketplaces alive with creativity' (*New Yorker*, 28 Sept 1982). Would only that it were so.

Credibility

Power to inspire confidence. Until the management/business world got its hands on the word, only events, actions and objects possessed credibility. People did not. During the 1960s, however, men and women in the USA were beginning to show signs of credibility, that is, their abilities inspired confidence in their fellow citizens and now, in the 1980s, there appear to be British people, too, who produce the same effect. Credibility has evidently become a highly marketable quality. Politicians yearn for it, salesmen have it, courses teach it, computers assess it. The person 'with a strong technical credibility' (*The Daily Telegraph*, 17 Sept 1981) is especially in demand.

Creme
Synthetic cream. In the UK, one may not advertise something as 'cream', unless it is derived from milk. For those who wish to sell a synthetic article, however, the problem can be solved by substituting 'creme' for 'cream'. 'Topped with whipped creme" (menu, Café Charco, Leicester Square, London, July 1982) probably illustrates this difference. One cannot be absolutely sure, however, since a certain amount of snobbery may be present in the situation, so that more 'cream' will be sold if it is spelt 'creme' or, better still, 'crème'. Different considerations apply to such compounds as 'salad cream' and 'shaving cream', which can and do contain no milk product whatever, without the slightest intention to deceive the customer.

'Creme' apart, the cream situation has become more than a little ridiculous in recent years, with strange commodities such as 'single cream', 'coffee cream', 'double cream', and even 'trifle cream' to confuse the judgement of the buyer and yield more profit to the gallon. Life was much easier when there was just 'cream'.

Crispy
Crisp. If one asks the average restaurateur exactly what the difference is between 'crisp' and 'crispy', he is likely to find himself somewhat at a loss for a convincing answer. He may say that 'crispy' is crispier than 'crisp', or that something which is 'crispy' is nicer, more appealing and more friendly than something which is merely 'crisp'. Pressed harder, he will say that 'crispy' is a better selling word, that it rolls over better in the mouth, that it causes the taste-buds to tingle faster and more vigorously. If he is unusually honest, he will admit that he does what everyone else does and that if 'crispy' happens to be the word of the moment, so be it. But very different kinds of crispiness can be involved. Once can have 'crispy lettuce hearts' (menu, Park Lane Hotel, London, July 1982) and 'crispy chicken wings' (menu, Garner's Steak House, Leicester Square, London, July 1982). There must be those who feel that 'crisp lettuce hearts' and 'crisp chicken wings' would indicate an establishment more to their taste and that plain 'lettuce' and 'chicken wings' would be better still. By their adjectives ye shall know them.

Culinary presentation
A meal prepared and arranged for the maximum visual effect, a dramatic buffet. This American institution, which now has a toe-hold in the UK, can be puzzling to those behind-the-scenes persons who

continue to think of food mainly as something to eat. A 'culinary presentation' is not at all the same as an attractively served meal. It is an occasion, planned and carried through by specialists, which uses dishes much as a mosaicist uses tesserae or a dress designer fabrics, playing one colour, shade and texture off against another. Such affairs can be very elaborate and very expensive, and they usually take place in a garden setting. It is possible to write of 'culinary presentations, as exciting as our water ski show' (*Florida Cyprus Gardens*, leaflet issued by the Cyprus Gardens Food Service, 1981). It is not forbidden to eat the food used for a culinary presentation 'once the applause has died down', but many people would feel a sense of desecration at doing so. If the play on words can be forgiven, 'culinary presentations' are in somewhat dubious taste and often approach the downright vulgar.

Currently
At the present time. The battle to prevent the importation of this Americanism into the UK has been fought and lost. The business world wanted it and the business world has got it, and perhaps it does not really matter very much if one says 'Currently the Joneses are running a Ford', instead of 'The Joneses are running a Ford at the moment'. What is still worth crusading against, however, is the increasingly common habit of introducing 'currently' into a sentence in order to give a bogus impression of immediacy, speed and activity. In such circumstances, it can usually be omitted altogether, without the slightest interference with the sense. In 'Currently we are substantially increasing our interests in the Middle East' (*The Daily Telegraph*, 17 Sept 1981), and 'We're currently looking for an independent man or woman aged 23+ with good secretarial skills' (*The Daily Telegraph*, 24 June 1982), the use of the present tense is sufficient indication that the increasing and looking are going on at this moment. The addition of 'currently' is made simply to prove what brisk, never-stopping concerns these are. Rather than a word to be put in, it is a word one dare not leave out, for fear of losing face among all the other 'currently' people.

Customer service
Protecting oneself against the misdeeds and bad habits of one's customers. This is a new and cynical meaning, a perhaps natural reaction against an over-used expression which had often proved itself to be little more than an empty shell. The implication is that in many cases the customers are not worth serving, a point one makes with the organ-

ization by standing the phrase on its head, as one sees in 'For six months they will be on "customer service" duties, a euphemism for catching fare-dodgers' (*The Sunday Times*, 17 Oct 1982).

D

Dedicated

Interested in the job. Once upon a time, it was possible to be 'dedicated' to one's work within only a very small range of occupations. Doctors and nurses were considered to be automatically 'dedicated' people, as were teachers and ministers of religion, and that, until about twenty years ago, was pretty well the lot. One was permitted to be 'dedicated', in other words, only if one belonged to a profession which one is supposed to exercise in the interests of humanity, and not primarily in order to make money. It is interesting to notice that lawyers and dentists have almost never been referred to as 'dedicated', which seems a little unfair.

Within recent years, however, the words has gone sadly downhill and nowadays almost anyone seems to feel entitled to think of themselves as 'dedicated'. In the engineering field one notices, for example, that 'candidates must be dedicated Service Engineers' (*The Daily Telegraph*, 7 Jan 1982) — the capital letters no doubt encourage the feeling of dedication — and a cruise company finds nothing ludicrous in advertising 'the heartwarming hospitality of the dedicated Italian crew' (*New York Times*, 17 Sept 1981), or a computer firm in saying of itself 'we're dedicated to expansion' (*The Daily Telegraph*, 17 Sept 1981), when all that is meant is something as crude and brutal as 'with us, it's expand or bust'.

Not infrequently, the use of 'dedicated' approaches the sickening, especially in the USA. Consider the case of the American psychologist whose patient had died as a result of her treatment. Her professional journal said that 'it felt sympathetic towards the psychologist, whom it had viewed as a sincere and dedicated person who had simply exhibited poor judgement' (*American Psychologist*, Dec 1981). How would one translate 'sincere and dedicated' here? 'Honest and extremely keen on her work'? 'Intelligent and hardworking'? Or are they, as seems very possible, simply woolly clichés, with no precise meaning at all, adjectives which automatically go with the job?

27

Dedication
Concentration, complete and never-faltering interest. As used and debased by the business world today, 'dedication' is nearly interchangeable with COMMITMENT. A more honest and sensible translation is always possible, although to insist on it often causes offence. In 'This dedication to quality at Ford Motor Company is paying off' (*New Yorker*, 17 May 1982), 'dedication' means 'unremitting attention', and so it does in 'Through our dedication to quality and customer service' (*The Daily Telegraph*, 26 Aug 1982). The following example, however, is a little more complicated. "At Mothercare,' says Joan, 'your place is on the sales floor with staff and customers. It's a job that demands dedication and total involvement." (*Scotsman*, 6 Nov 1981). The paragon, or idiot, described here is the person in charge of the chain of Mothercare shops, which, one should perhaps add for the benefit of posterity, sell clothes and equipment for mothers, prospective mothers, babies and small children. There must surely be something seriously wrong with anyone who is willing to give the whole of their energy, thinking and waking hours to such a job, however, important it may be to the wellbeing of the nation. Yet 'dedication and total involvement' can mean no less.

Behind the word 'dedication' lie two concepts, both of which are unpleasant and inhuman. The first is that business is some kind of religious activity and the second is that, just as it is fitting for a person to devote his life entirely to the service of God, so it is entirely right and proper and indeed a privilege for a man to devote his entire life and personality to furthering the cause of a business, forswearing all other pursuits and interests. It is this monstrous idea which has made 'dedication' so important in industry and commerce and which demands never-ending exposure for the fraud and Black Mass it is.

Demanding
Exhausting. The more dreadful the economic situation becomes, the harder companies push their sales staff, always with the background threat of 'If you won't or can't work under this pressure, there are plenty of others who would love to step into your shoes'. The realities of the job are never, however, spelt out in their brutal awfulness. The technique is to present the selling of petfood, shoes or whatever as if it were an Antarctic expedition or an army survival course, a test of one's strength stamina and manhood, which one is privileged to undergo. The morale-building language is of this kind — 'Only those prepared to accept the rigours of speciality selling need apply for these extremely demanding

position' (*The Daily Telegraph*, 26 Aug 1982), a free translation of which might be 'Only those willing to kill themselves in our service need apply'.

Designer

Designed by a professional. A house can possess, for example, 'a designer lounge with woodburning fireplace' (*New Yorker*, 14 June 1982). This is very similar to the house itself being described as 'architect designed', and illustrates precisely the same swindle. What matters is not the fact that the house is 'architect designed' or has 'a designer lounge', but whether the architect or designer is any good. The implication that all designers and architects are talented, even brilliant, and that to employ one is to guarantee oneself satisfaction in advance is as ludicrous as pretending that all doctors or lawyers are equally competent. But the myth, naturally, is one which the professions themselves are extremely anxious to encourage.

Desirable

Highly praised by agents, popularized. Houses have been 'desirable' for many years, often without the slightest justification and whole areas, both at home and abroad, are liable to receive the same treatment nowadays. A property agent will refer, for example, to 'the most desirable location of the Costa del Sol' (*Sunday Telegraph*, 24 Jan 1982). The technique is ultimately self-defeating, although it succeeds well enough for a while. First, the area is publicized as 'desirable' and, in the early stages, it often is, because it has so far escaped vandalization and devastation and has a number of pleasant natural amenities. As a result of the developers' efforts, so many people find it officially 'desirable' that it ceases to be desirable in any way at all and it begins to go socially and financially downhill, as the same kind of residents embark on leap-frogging operations in order to discover another area elsewhere, where the rape of the landscape is still in its preliminary stages. Prospective purchasers consequently need to decide very quickly at which stage of desirability their chosen spot is. Is it in Phase One, still largely unspoilt, or in Phase Two, effectively ruined, but fashionable, or in Phase Three, when the original inhabitants, having seen through the swindle, are being replaced by people of lesser status, who have come simply for the sun, the sea and the golf course, and who are soon going to become very bored when they realise this is all they have bought?

Dialogue
Talk, interchange of ideas. A new favourite of the world of management. A typical instance of this sparkling addition to the word stock of such people is 'Constant dialogue is exchanged between our Marketing Department and Sales Representatives' (*Scotsman*, 6 Nov 1981). The use of capital letters should be noted (*see* CAPITALS, USE OF), and the whole sentence is a masterpiece of the unnecessary, a wonderful example of how to fill expensive space to no purpose. It amounts to saying that members of the firm's marketing and sales departments are on speaking terms with one another and are in the habit of talking over common problems, to reveal which there seems to be little point in devoting part of the annual advertising budget.

Dimension
An element, quality. Length, breadth and height are dimensions and way beyond them is the Fourth Dimension of time, and it is not easy to see how one's life or career can be seen in quite these terms. Yet the advertisers are constantly urging us to add a new dimension to our lives by buying this or doing that and firms feel able to assure prospective applicants for positions with them that 'You'll add an exciting new dimension to your career' (*New York Times*, 27 Sept 1981). Which of the four dimensions this is to be, or whether it is a fifth or a sixth, unknown to physics, is never specified. But there is evidently something prestigious and stimulating about a dimension, something which only business initiates understand.

Discipline
A subject. The word is beloved of non-scientific academics, in their never-ending attempt to make their subjects as prestigious and fundworthy as those practised by their scientific colleagues. 'Subject' has become old-fashioned, if not positively dangerous, because it suggests an easy-going, pleasure-seeking attitude to one's work, far removed from the we-toil-in-the-nation's-interest approach of the physicists and engineers. 'Discipline' is an invaluable tool in the battle for recognition and esteem, with its monastic, self-sacrificing overtones and its strong hint that every penny is being well-spent. RIGOROUS is part of the same battle-pack.

So we find one university department seeking a recruit who will be 'able to contribute to the work of the Psychology discipline' (*The Guardian*, 2 Feb 1982) and another casting its net wide for a researcher, who 'will also undertake some teaching in his/her own discipline' (*The*

Guardian, 2 Feb 1982). Ten years ago it would still have been possible to undertake some teaching in one's own subject, but today a subject-person would be considered a mere dilettante, spiritually and theologically weak. But what exactly is one to understand by 'Candidates should be proven all-rounders in the discipline' (*The Daily Telegraph*, 18 Feb 1982)? The great essential in today's academic world is that one's specialism shall be as sharp and small as the point of a pin. How does an all-rounder maintain his balance or even survive on that small space? What sort of super athlete is this?

Discreet

Not too obvious. Those who market perfumes to be used by men have above-average problems to overcome. If the stuff smells of nothing, there is no point in buying it but, if its presence is too obvious, the treasured macho image is in peril. So the choice of the right adjectives in the advertising matter is more than important. It is crucial. After much trial and error, and no doubt hours of discussion behind locked doors, Dior settled for this, at least for the time being — 'Virile. Discreet. Refreshing. Uncompromising' (*New Yorker*, 14 June 1982). What precisely this adds up to, no-one can say, and certainly one is not meant to ask. But just how something can be both 'discreet' and 'uncompromising' at the same time is not clear.

Double

Two, twice the usual size, twice the usual strength or consistency. This is a much-used food word and one to approach with great caution. One is offered, for example, 'double cream', without being given the slightest idea of what it is. 'Double' what? Thick cream, sir. But how thick? Ah, you must buy it and see, sir. And so on. We are back to our old friend the oilier oil. The fact of the matter is that 'double cream' is what used once to be sold as 'cream', and a miserable thing called 'coffee cream', little better than thickened milk, has appeared, to take care of the bottom end of the market.

One is also confronted with a mysterious object known as a 'double lamb chop', which careful research shows to be a single chop, thicker than normal, as a result of having two ribs of the sheep instead of one, in it. If one is really favoured, one may find both 'double cream' and a 'double lamb chop' on the same restaurant menu — 'Black or white with double cream', and 'Double lamb chop. A tender cut across the loin' (Myllet Arms, Perivale, Middlesex, England, July 1982).

Dynamic
Full of activity. This old-established nuisance may just possibly be about to retreat to the back of the industrial/commercial stage, having occupied a footlights position for far longer than it ever deserved. The sign of weakening prestige is the introduction of another heavily charged word to support it — 'your immediate prospects in a dynamic growth environment' (*The Sunday Times*, 25 Oct 1981). At one time, 'dynamic' would always have been strong enough to stand on its own, but it could be that the world has grown tired of perpetual dynamism and longs for a little peace and constructive thinking. But, in its days of glory, 'dynamic' has done a lot of harm, over-stressing and over-valuing perpetual movement and change and the people who exemplify it, so that energy has come to be considered a virtue in its own right, irrespective of the ends to which it is directed. A 'dynamic growth environment' could well be one to avoid, with everyone so busy growing that life and civilization pass them by. And exactly what dynamic tax advisers get up to is known only to their employers and themselves, but such people certainly exist, because 'The opportunity has arisen for a senior tax adviser to work as part of a small dynamic team' (*The Sunday Times*, 25 Oct 1981). One can only suppose that they advise dynamically, but that really takes us little further forward.

E

Echelon
Section, level. The love of industrial management for military terminology is insatiable, partly, no doubt, because most managing directors are generals who have missed their vocation. So beans are baked, cars assembled and clothing stitched in an atmosphere of lines of command, *X* reporting to *Y*, and taking of leave, which, at least in theory, lets everyone know exactly where he stands and how far he can go. 'Echelon' has now arrived, to stiffen the morale of the industrial officer class, and recruits with the necessary force of character are required 'to strengthen a vital engineering management echelon' (*The Daily Telegraph*, 18 Feb 1982).

Economical
Cheap, low. These are, however, words which are likely to get one banished from polite society for ever, in a world in which cheap has become synonymous with nasty, except among the young, who are lucky enough not to have reached the age where these things matter. So, to prospective advertisers, one may not say that one's rates are 'low' or 'cheap', for fear of causing all decent people to run fast in the opposite direction. It has to be 'Rates are pleasingly economical' (*New York Times*, 27 Sept 1981).

But to use 'economical' in this cowardly fashion is to make it increasingly difficult to maintain a good word in the station to which it is accustomed. Nowadays, in these hard-up times, one needs the real 'economical' more than ever. It is 'economical' to make soup out of bones, 'economical' to tie up one's roses with strips of discarded tights, 'economical' to re-use old envelopes. One must not allow such a morale-raising word to be taken over by the Devil. *See also* BUDGET.

Engaged
Having strong views on something, partisan, identified with a cause. The *roman engagé* has been a recognized literary genre for several genera-

33

tions and a literal translation was inevitable, since it appeared, to those who knew little French, to echo the original so beautifully, the fact that '*engagé*' has subtleties which are not the same as those of 'engaged' being immaterial.

Having acquired the word as part of their professional stock-in-trade, British and American reviewers and critics do some decidedly strange things with it. What, for instance, is one to make of a novel which is described as 'engaged and detached, funny and sad' (*New Yorker*, 20 Sept 1982)? If it is 'engaged', with what is it engaged, and if it is 'detached', from what is it detached? One is not told. It is clearly sufficient to be 'engaged', just as it is to be AWARE or CARING.

Enhance

To make better, improve. Or at least this is what the word means to the literate among us. Many of our fellow citizens, however, especially in the business world, are not literate, although they may be numerate and possess many other talents and perhaps even virtues. *The Dictionary of Diseased English* contained the noun, 'enhancement', but not the verb, and commented that it was 'a new favourite in the business world'. Since then, matters have got seriously out of hand and it is often difficult to decide now what either the noun or the verb is supposed to mean. A sentence for advanced students is 'We are seeking to enhance our Sales Management team with more thoroughly professional direct sales people' (*Daily Express*, 11 Feb 1982). The student is asked to decide whether the firm wishes to (*a*) improve the quality of its sales management team by injecting into it some people who are more thoroughly professional than those already there, or (*b*) enlarge the team by adding some more thorough professionals to the thorough professionals who are employed at the moment.

'You will also be responsible for the recommendation of enhanced recovery schemes' (*The Daily Telegraph*, 18 Feb 1982) would appear on the face of it to be using 'enhanced' in the traditional and correct sense of 'improved', although one cannot be absolutely sure, and one wonders in any case why this Canadian petrochemical concern fought shy of 'improved' or 'more efficient', which would have put the matter beyond doubt.

Enviable

Better than average. So far as estate agents are concerned, the Seven Deadly Sins and the Ten Commandments went by the board years ago and yesterday's sins and vices are today's virtues. The point was made in

The Dictionary of Diseased English, when 'enviable' was a recent addition to the everyday vocabulary of the business world. It has now acquired something of a period flavour, but it is widely used, although just how much it contributes to the selling of houses is difficult to say. The probability is that the estate agents appreciate it more than their clients do. How many people in search of a new Somerset home are more likely to buy a particular property if it is described as 'This enviable 4-year-old house' (*Western Gazette*, 4 June 1982) or if it contains '2 spacious recep., cloakroom, enviable kitchen' (*Western Gazette*, 4 June 1982)? One will never know for sure, but the betting is that the word 'enviable' has not influenced the deal in the slightest.

But if it has to be something from the envy stable, 'enviable' does at least make sense, which is more than can be said for 'envious'. The firm which 'has an envious record as one of Australia's leading exporters of defence equipment' (*The Daily Telegraph*, 3 Nov 1981) may have little to learn about grammar, but it would do itself no harm by adding one or two literate people to its staff, able at least to distinguish between 'envious' and 'enviable'. The situation is made even worse when we are told that 'the company's growth is due largely to its professionalism'. Modesty is no bad thing on occasions. It is important, by the way, to point out that in this particular instance the advertisement was inserted in the paper by the company itself, not by a recruitment agency. There is no buck to pass.

Environment

Any place of work, especially a factory. *The Dictionary of Diseased English* pointed out, in suggesting this definition, that 'factory' had become a very dirty word indeed among those who earned a living on the upper levels of management and that 'environment' had become the favourite euphemism. The word is still widely used in this sense. People continue to be required 'with at least 5 years experience in an appropriate mass production environment' (*The Daily Telegraph*, 6 Jan 1982), and 'a minimum of 2-3 years experience in a medium or large-scale environment' (*New York Times*, 27 Sept 1981), and there are 'challenging management roles in an established unionised environment' (*The Daily Telegraph*, 18 Feb 1982).

Very often nowadays 'environment' appears to have been inserted simply on the grounds that no sentence is complete without it, even though it carries no meaning whatever. Examples abound — 'Previous experience of corporate planning environment is desirable' (*The Sunday Times*, 25 Oct 1981); 'experience in a food production environment' (*The Daily Telegraph*, 19 Feb 1982); 'an estimator with 3-plus years experience, preferably in a machine-shop environment' (*Boston Globe*, 11 Oct 1981); 'three to seven years in military environment logic design' (*The Sunday Times*, 25 Oct 1981).

Sometimes 'environment' is the wrong word to convey the desired meaning. The company looking for 'a qualified engineer with solid management experience, preferably in a multinational environment' (*The Daily Telegraph*, 1 Dec 1981) wants a man used to working with a mixed nationality labour force, and 'the new environment' for which 'a number of high calibre systems programmers' are needed is really a new department or new section of the business.

Now and again 'environment' appears to be a synonym for 'job' or 'conditions of the job' — 'Rewards are commensurate with the pressures of this environment' (*The Daily Telegraph*, 26 Aug 1982) and possibly, too, 'a fast-moving, highly challenging environment' (*The Daily Telegraph*, 5 Nov 1981). But precisely how an 'environment' can be 'aggressive and forthright' is not at all clear. Yet such curiosities evidently do occur, since a company tells its prospective paragons that 'You must be capable of managing operations in an aggressive and forthright environment' (*The Daily Telegraph*, 15 Dec 1981). It is possible that in this case 'environment' means 'colleagues' or 'employees'. *See also* FACILITY and LOCATION.

Essential engineering

Engineering. 'Essential engineering' is a curious phrase, extensively used by British Rail and by nobody else. It was coined in a misguided attempt to soften the wrath of passengers who find their trains delayed as a result of permanent way repairs and renewals. The idea is presumably that 'essential engineering' and its consequences will be readily excused by the travelling public, whereas mere 'engineering' might be considered wilful and a luxury, set in motion expressly for the purpose of annoying and inconveniencing passengers. Instructions have therefore gone out that the style shall be 'The delay has been caused by essential engineering work near Exeter' (British Rail announcement, Temple Meads station, Bristol, England 1 Dec 1982). *See also* PREVENTIVE MAINTENANCE.

Ethical

Advertised only in professional publications and, as a general rule, not available to the general public without a prescription. This extraordinary term, in use since the mid-1930s, was discussed fairly fully in *The*

Dictionary of Diseased English, and the situation has changed very little in the meantime, at least so far as pharmaceutical products destined for human beings are concerned. Nowadays, however, it plays a not inconsiderable part in the veterinary world, too. A salesman may be told that, in order to qualify for the job, he needs to have 'several years' experience of small and large ethical animal products' (*The Daily Telegraph*, 18 Feb 1982).

The use of 'ethical' in this sense would seem to be not without certain dangers. If the goods which the public cannot buy freely are 'ethical', there must always be a nasty suspicion that what can be obtained without any trouble must be in some way 'unethical', and that is hardly an idea which either the manufacturer or the shopkeeper would like to encourage.

Excess
'In excess of' means 'more than', but some strange mental block appears to prevent many businessmen from using the everyday expression, so that we are told instead, not very grammatically, about 'an organisation in excess of fifty people' (*The Daily Telegraph*, 2 June 1982). There is little doubt that, for the concern in question, to have 'in excess of fifty people' makes it feel more important and perhaps even bigger than to have 'more than fifty people', although those outside this strange world may well wonder just why this should be so. There may also be a suggestion that 'in excess of' is scientific and accurate, in a way that 'more' is not, although there is no logic whatever behind this. The fundamental reason for choosing 'in excess of' is, alas, the pomposity and formality which hang over industry and commerce like a thick fog.

Exciting
Interesting, novel. People, as one should know, come in many different kinds and excitement can have some strange causes. There must surely, however, be something a little odd or even perverted about a person who can be turned on by a roof. Yet 'an exciting flat-roof insulation system' (*The Daily Telegraph*, 10 Dec 1981) compels one to admit that such things can be so. But, by using a strong word like 'exciting', when a lower-key is really called for, one is creating unnecessary difficulties for oneself. If 'exciting' has already been reserved for such a matter of fact affair as an insulation system, what is left when something genuinely emotion-stirring comes along?

Exclusive

The Dictionary of Diseased English defines this, cynically but perfectly reasonably, as 'expensive'. With hindsight and as a result of letters received — some of them decidedly petulant — it would seem wise to expand this to 'expensive and fashionable'. That done, it needs to be noted, if only for the benefit of posterity, that snobbery is as powerful a social force in the UK and the USA in 1983 as it was in 1977 and that the idea of possessing something which only 5 per cent of one's fellow citizens at most can afford is still immensely attractive. Those with goods and services to sell consequently do well to continue to regard 'exclusive' as a valuable property and to urge the right kind of people to 'linger over cocktails in our exclusive VIP lounge' (*New Yorker*, 18 Oct 1981) and, by buying a house wisely, to discover 'an exclusive way of life on an historic Bristol waterway' (*Bristol Evening Post*, 24 June 1982).

To use 'exclusive' in this way now is an old-established Anglo-Saxon custom and it is going to take some shifting, even if one saw any point in making the effort. But the concept of exclusivity can be carried a little too far for comfort and understanding. What, for instance, is one to make of 'America's most exclusive line of liquid aluminium' (*Sunday Telegraph*, 6 June 1982)? It is difficult to see how snobbery and fashion can be extended to take in liquid aluminium. Does 'exclusive' in this context mean, perhaps, that this wonderful material is made by only one firm or distributed through only one supplier? If not, what does it mean? Perhaps aluminium is more fashionable than one realizes.

Executive

Higher salaried. Everything that needs to be said about this ridiculous word can be found in *The Dictionary of Diseased English*. There are fortunately signs that the fashion for it is declining, especially as an adjective. The last people to be found using it will probably be provincial estate agents, who still believe that it adds a touch of class to an otherwise undistinguished house. 100 miles from London one can find plenty of examples of 'this executive-style five year-old Det. House' (*Western Gazette*, 3 March 1982), but in the Home Counties of England, with executives so thick on the ground, the word is no longer worth using.

Experience

To feel, undergo. Only living creatures can have experiences. Industrial concerns cannot feel or breathe, so they cannot experience anything. But it is a nice long word, good for padding out a sentence, so in it goes, meaning or no meaning, as in 'General Electric is currently experiencing a rapid expansion of its European activities' (*The Daily Telegraph*, 18 Feb 1982). This could be translated as 'General Electric is expanding its European activities', but that, presumably, is not reckoned to catch public attention as much as the image of the electrical giant flexing his muscles across Europe and enjoying the feeling. But such a poetic concept may flatter the journalist who wrote the sentence.

Exposure
Experience. This extraordinary new sense of 'exposure' first appeared on the scene in the mid-1970s. It has all the feeling of an innovation made by someone with an imperfect knowledge of English, possibly a recent Bulgarian immigrant to the USA. In its ineptness, it reminds one strongly of the old proverb, 'You can take a horse to the water, but you cannot make him drink'. A colour-blind person can be 'exposed' to a dozen Picassos, but it is doubtful if he will profit a great deal from the activity. 'Exposure' and 'experience' simply are not and cannot be synonyms, however hard and obstinately the business world may try. 'Experience of computers' makes perfect sense, and so does 'previous general experience of the Food/Grocery market', but 'no previous exposure to computers is assumed' (*New York Times*, 27 Sept 1981) and 'You should be in your mid-thirties and with previous general exposure to the Food/Grocery market' (*The Sunday Times*, 14 March 1982) are simply wilful idiocy, and they could well be confusing into the bargain, since there are possibly people with suitable experience who may feel that, because they are not conscious of having had exposure, they would not be considered for the job.

F

Face to face communication
Talk, conversation, discussion. Things have come to a pretty pass when one feels compelled to find a more impressive equivalent of 'talk', and to a state of high farce when applicants for a managerial post have to be told, or at any rate, are told that 'the ability to handle face to face communication with many different kinds of people is of major importance' (*The Daily Telegraph*, 10 June 1982). Old-time industrial managers, well used to confrontation and argument, would have found this both ludicrous and unbelievable. What kind of firm, they would have wanted to know, would employ managers without the words or the confidence to talk to their colleagues and subordinates? Not long ago the phrase was 'must be able to communicate well'. We have evidently gone downhill even further since then. What, we may well ask, have the business schools been doing if they have been turning out, year after year, highly trained people who cannot talk?

Facility
Lavatory, factory, hospital, office block, shop. 'Facility' is rapidly becoming the supreme all-purpose euphemism, often for objects or places which do not, at first sight, appear to stand in any particular need of a euphemism. The context will usually make the meaning clear, although sometimes a little ingenuity may be required and now and again, where a mistranslation would be disastrous, special care is to be recommended.

In 'Simpson Europe Ltd., with its European facility at Shannon, Ireland' (*The Birmingham Post*, 5 Nov 1981), a factory is referred to, and this is also the case with 'To work on facilities equipment associated with chemical manufacturers' processes' (*The Daily Telegraph*, 7 Jan 1982), and 'Being located in Jeddah at a brand-new facility' (*The Daily Telegraph*, 7 Jan 1982). 'The largest European production facility within this substantial U.S. corporation' (*The Sunday Times*, 25 Oct 1981) adds 'production' for safety, in case some ill-informed readers should think that the corporation was accommodated in a lavatory or a hospital. A hospital it really is in 'A psychiatric facility known for excellence' (*New Yorker*, 29 June 1981), and a lavatory, probably with a shower included, in 'All cabins have private facilities' (*New Yorker*, 19 Oct 1981).

A 'facility' can be a shop or showroom, good honest words which were once used with pride, but which now require veneering — 'Our entire stock of Handmade Oriental Designer Area Rugs and Remnants will be moved to a completely new and larger facility' (*The Daily Telegraph*, 14 Jan 1982); 'this exciting new office facility' (*Boston Globe*, 11 Oct 1981) — and this EXCITING new office facility is concerned with nothing more exciting than an office block, but if 'building' is felt to be less everyday and drab than 'block', then so be it. 'Facility' is an obligingly flexible word, allowing for all shades of meaning and all overtones. It must be a very strong candidate for inclusion in any up-to-date list of the 100 most essential words of today's basic English. *See also* ENVIRONMENT and LOCATION.

Family

Well-to-do middle class. This very popular, but reassuringly vague estate agents' word could land foreigners in difficulties. One has to know and understand English extremely well in order to be sensitive to its full possibilities. 'A family house of immense character' (*Country Life*, 21 May 1981) provides a basis of a definition. One could usefully begin by explaining that although most British families live in houses, they do not live in family houses, a curious fact which the conventional dictionary does not make clear or even hint at. A 'family house', as the estate agents use the term, is a large, solidly-built detached house, with at least four bedrooms and surrounded by a large garden, in which children can run around, play games and climb trees. Perhaps half of one per cent of families in the UK are rich and fortunate enough to possess such a house.

One would certainly need to have quite a lot of money in order to be in a position to buy a 'superbly modernised and luxuriously appointed house on the edge of Richmond Park, offering exceptional family accommodation on two floors' (advertisement by Friend and Falke, *London Property*, mid-Jan 1983). It should be noted that in London, and only in London, 'families' are permitted to occupy flats. Elsewhere, there are only 'family houses'. This is because London has, if one can afford the frightening price, a fair number of large, 'family sized' flats, which are sometimes advertised in rather strange terms, such as 'The flat provides well-decorated family accommodation' (advertisement by

Ridley and Company, *London Portrait,* Jan 1983). One evidently has to distinguish between mere 'family accommodation', which is expensive, and 'well-decorated family accommodation', which is even more expensive.

Equally in need of explanation is the 'family estate', as illustrated by 'quite superb small family estate' (*Country Life*, 21 May 1981), This will, of course, be attached to a 'family house' and it will almost certainly be either in the country or on the extreme suburban edge of a large town. It will contain between two and four acres, so providing grazing for at least one pony or horse, and its social cachet is considerably increased by a portion of woodland. The proportion of British families with a 'family estate' of this kind is infinitesimal, which greatly increases its desirability and prestige.

Farmhouse
Made on the farm, from milk produced on the same farm. Would only that it were so. The reality behind 'farmhouse butter' and 'farmhouse cheese' is rather different. Both are now usually little more than romantic expressions retained for their commercial usefulness among city dwellers, for whom 'farmhouse' evokes images of Devonshire teas, apple-faced women and fresh foodstuffs tasting of something, and in this sense the word is an amiable but astute fraud. Very little English cheese or butter is made either in the farmhouse or by traditional methods nowadays. Those farmers who turn their milk into butter or cheese do so on a factory scale, tons every week, and with equipment and techniques which are little or no different from those employed by big commercial concerns, like Unigate. What they sell is factory produce, not farmhouse produce. If they are very large dairy farmers indeed, a high proportion of the milk they use may come from their own cows, but even then they are likely to buy in substantial quantities from other farmers. Any idea that 'farmhouse' means 'lovingly and patiently produced in small quantities' is a complete myth. 'Fresh Milk for Farmhouse Cheese', a big Somerset cheesemaking concern announces to the world on its tanker lorries (seen near Castle Cary, 27 Dec 1982, and on hundreds of other occasions in many other places). All it means is 'Milk for Cheese', but that has no romantic, buttercups and milkmaid associations at all.

Fast-footed
Rapidly expanding, leaving one's competitors behind. The past five years has produced a crop of these 'fast' compounds, all equally tedious and bogus. The idea is presumably to generate a feeling that business is a

high-speed drama, a never-ending Olympic Games in which competitors, inside and outside the firm, exist only to be outrun and
defeated. It is therefore possible to talk and write, without even a vestige
of a smile, of 'the success and control of fast-footed organisations' (*The
Sunday Times*, 25 Oct 1981). There is still some hope left, however.
One has yet to hear someone saying at a party that he works for a fast-
footed organization. Self-respect and a sense of the ridiculous are not
completely dead, even in commercial and industrial circles.

Fast on one's feet

Quick thinking and quick acting, energetic. The expression is part of the
jargon of modern management of the slicker and more suspect kind,
where really powerful and important people have on their desks printed
notices saying 'Tortoises not wanted here', and similar invigorating
thoughts. Someone willing and eager to become Marketing Manager,
Toiletries — a post and a function not, it might be suggested, of outstanding national importance — is therefore told, with somewhat
creaking grammar, 'You will therefore be someone who is fast on your
(*sic*) feet and thrives on challenges' (*The Daily Telegraph*, 24 June
1982). For the benefit of those whose mind moves more easily towards
cynical definitions of strange expressions, it should be emphasized that a
person who is 'fast on his feet' is not someone who finds it difficult to get
out of the job quickly enough.

Fast-paced

High pressured, ruthless, sink-or-swim. Most modern businesses are
not, in actual fact, characterized by the break-neck speed at which they
get things done but, in order to maintain the firm's reputation, it is
necessary to present a fast front to the world. One of the ways in which
this is achieved is to apply adjectives like 'fast-paced' to oneself at every
possible opportunity. So one tells new recruits that they will be working
'in a fast-paced environment' (*Boston Globe*, 11 Oct 1981) or that 'the
environment is challenging, fast-paced and rewarding' (*New York
Times*, 27 Sept 1981). It is highly flattering, if not always true.

Fast track

First-class, successful. A new woolly word, which means very little but is
now enormously used in the business world. The 'track' is presumably an
assembly-line conveyor, so that to be 'fast track' is to move fast, to get
ahead. As with so many new pieces of management jargon, however,
this one is used almost automatically by those who feel obliged to prove

that they are up with the industrial commandos. One should not look too closely for any precise meaning in it, but it is sometimes possible to substitute 'bright' or 'outstanding' and produce a sensible sentence from the result. 'Outstanding' would look reasonably well with 'If you have a fast track career ...' (*New York Times*, 27 Sept 1981), and 'We hire fast-track, aggressive people' (*Boston Globe*, 11 Oct 1981). But a firm which actually got a 'fast track self-starter' (*New York Times*, 27 Sept 1981) might possibly come to regret its choice.

Feature
Dominating, unable to be ignored. This is a very ingenious estate agents' word, which can be of considerable help in desperate situations, when something urgent has to be done about a particularly hideous, inconvenient or out-of-scale item in the architecture or interior arrangements of a house. At one stroke, it is converted from an embarrassment into a 'feature'. One is offered, for example, a 'feature fireplace' (*Bristol Evening Post*, 24 June 1982) as yet another reason for buying the property. Experience of other 'feature fireplaces', however, gives one a pretty good idea of what this particular one is going to look like. If it is Victorian or Edwardian, it will look rather as if it had formed part of the fittings of a good-class grocer's shop of the period, with a superabundance of shelving and mirrors above and a prodigious amount to keep clean down below. If it is modern, it will be of the baronial proportions which demand a room at least four times the size, and will contain the kind of Disneyland brick or stonework which causes any sensitive person to feel immediately faint. In nine cases out of ten 'features' are not a good thing.

Fine
Best quality, high class. The Americans and the British do not use 'fine' in the same way, and this can be a source of considerable confusion, especially since in both countries the word often does not mean very much. There is, of course, no trouble when 'fine' is used in such contexts as 'fine weather', 'fine breadcrumbs', or 'fine brush'. The difficulties begin only when 'fine' becomes a value word and then only because Americans find it so difficult to say 'good', 'better' or 'best'. One or two examples will illustrate the problem. What does an American mean when he says 'I am a frequent traveller and a patron of finer hotels' (*New Yorker*, 17 May 1982)? Why does he say 'finer' and not 'fine' or 'the finest'? How should one translate 'finer' for the benefit of a British

public? 'Above average'? 'The better type of'? 'Expensive, but not the most expensive'? 'Quiet and refined'?

Similar questions suggest themselves in the case of 'Fine dining is provided in the La Sala and El Portico dining rooms' (town brochure from Scottsdale, Arizona, 1982). Does one interpret this as 'elegant', 'refined', 'provided food and wine of good quality', or 'snobbish'? And, if we are told of a hotel in Florida that is 'where the finest guests meet' (*New York Times*, 27 Sept 1981), what would we expect to find if fate should take us there? Rich people? Socially elevated people? Exceptionally well dressed and well mannered people?

Life is no easier with this tantalizing word when one moves away from people. What, for example, is 'a fine whole fish, carefully selected and grilled' (menu, Myllet Arms, Perivale, Middlesex, England, July 1982)? A big fish? A fish in choice condition? A beautiful-looking fish? If communication is one's aim, 'fine' could be a good word to avoid.

Finished
Painted, decorated. *The Dictionary of Diseased English* noted this use of the word in connection with restaurant food, where it means 'accompanied with' — 'finished in a sherry sauce' — and superior motorcars — 'finished in Seychelles blue with beige hide upholstery'. The habit has now spread to the house agents, who also use 'finished' as a sure sign of class — 'A beautiful second floor pied-à-terre, finished to the highest standards' (advertisement by Ann McKee and Company, *London Property*, mid-Jan 1983). A council house would be painted or decorated, never finished.

Fiscal
Financial. This remarkable American euphemism has not yet crossed the Atlantic and with reasonable luck it can be held at bay for a year or two longer. It originated within the American medical profession, which for some time has been rather more concerned with money than is fitting among those who have taken the Hippocratic oath, and some of its contexts are likely to seem very strange indeed to the simple British. Talk of 'the ambiguity in the psychiatrist's fiscal relationship to individual patients' (*American Journal of Psychiatry*, 138, 12 Dec 1981) is likely to be largely meaningless here and may not be much better understood by quite a few Americans, too. Except in so far as his income and the taxes he pays are closely linked, neither a psychiatrist nor any other kind of doctor can have a 'fiscal' relationship with his patients, although in the USA he will certainly be on close financial terms with them.

Fly
To go, travel. Journalists love 'fly', partly because it is very short and partly because it adds, or is supposed to add, speed, urgency and vividness to the story. So it is always found necessary to say that someone 'flew' from New York to London, even though it is extremely unlikely that he would have travelled in any other way. All this flying takes place just as frequently in broadcast news bulletins as in newspapers — 'A delegation of Spanish bishops is flying to Rome today' (BBC Radio 4, 5 Sept 1982); 'He flies to South Africa on Tuesday' (BBC Radio 4, 10 July 1982); 'Two officers of the Royal Ulster Constabulary flew to London from Belfast' (BBC Radio 4, 31 Oct 1982). There are times when one feels that all long-distance travellers have sprouted wings and turned into birds. How refreshing it would be to hear it said of a cricketer, or indeed of anyone else, that 'He is going to South Africa on Tuesday'. How it would seize our attention.

Foursquare
Solid and uncomplicated. This definition is, alas, no more than a guess. 'Foursquare' is one of those words of which wine experts will say, in the most infuriating way imaginable, 'I can't explain it. You either know what it means or you don't.' What one is supposed to do if one is unfortunate enough to belong to the second category is not made clear. But here is the knowledgeable men's term in its context: 'Definite, foursquare, somewhat lacking in bouquet to many European tastes' (*The Times*, 31 Oct 1981).

Fourstar
Good and expensive. 'America's only four-star steak and seafood restaurant' (*New Yorker*, 17 May 1982) is as meaningless as the advertisements of a thousand other restaurants around the world which award themselves stars in a great flurry of self-congratulation and then expect the eating public to believe them. No star is worth anything unless one knows who gave it and what the organization's criteria were, which is another way of saying that nearly all star-ratings should be thrown straight into the wastepaper-basket.

Freshly
Just for you, cooked today for the first time. Restaurants have become indecently fond of telling their customers that this or that dish is 'freshly' cooked. One's instinct is to retaliate by saying 'So it should be', but that would spoil the game and interfere with the innocent pleasure of people

at neighbouring tables. However, even if one keeps one's doubts and rage to oneself when presented with the menu, a little quiet reflection is perfectly in order. Consider, for example, 'a heap of freshly baked pork ribs' (Tennessee Pancake House, Leicester Square, London, July 1982). 'Heap' can be disregarded for the moment — how many pork ribs go to the heap and are they deposited on the plate with a shovel? — and there is no reason to draw attention to the fact that a London restaurant is using the American 'baked', instead of the English, 'roast'. The key word here is 'freshly'. If one's pork ribs are placed on the table at 1.15 pm, how many hours or minutes before that time did they first go into the oven? Was it the same day at all, or perhaps the day before? Are they freshly baked or freshly reheated? 'Freshly' can mean very different things to different people and it is as well to be on one's guard.

Full-course

All the courses one expects or wants. For those not in the know, this must surely be one of the most baffling restaurant innovations of all time. Without a personal computer, how does one decide the meaning of 'Three delicious full-course meals served daily' (*New York Times*, 27 Sept 1981)? The first task, evidently, is to come to grips with 'full-course meals'. Do such meals contain three courses, four courses or what? Are they perhaps meals made up of one single enormous course, 'a full-course'? And are three of these meals all available at the same time, say at lunch? Or is one offered one for breakfast, another for lunch, and a third for dinner? How hungry should one arrive at the restaurant?

Function

Department, section. How and why 'function' came to be used in this ridiculous sense is a mystery. In 1977 *The Dictionary of Diseased English* reported that 'function' had become 'one of the three most loved words of today's industrial world'. Now, in 1983, it would probably be necessary to say 'one of the six most loved words', not because 'function' is less used than previously, but because the amount of prestigious, ungrammatical rubbish has increased so alarmingly. There is no doubt at all that, away from a handful of sensible, respectable firms like Marks and Spencer, to talk of 'departments' is to admit publicly that one belongs to yesterday. So one finds that 'Personal development will not be confined to the function you join' (*Sunday Telegraph*, 6 June 1982), and hears of 'a new post resulting from a reorganisation of the Engineering Function' (*The Sunday Times*, 25 Oct 1981). But one does not join a function: one has a function and what has been reorganized is not and cannot be the engineering function, but the engineering department, the function of which can only be engineering. Who, one might well ask, would want to join such a vague, cold abstraction as a function, when one could have the humanity and reality of a department?

Functional
Departmental. One can say of something which is badly designed or which refuses to work properly that it is not 'functional', or of someone doing the work of the managing director, while that person was away ill, that he was the 'functional managing director'. But, as a result of the absurd use of FUNCTION, one is never quite sure nowadays what, if anything, 'functional' is supposed to mean, at least in the world of business. Suppose, for instance, that someone is required to have had 'a minimum of 3-5 years' experience as the functional head of sales' (*The Daily Telegraph*, 17 Sept 1981). What, one then asks, is the difference between 'head of sales' and 'functional head of sales'? The answer is 'absolutely nothing'. No concern that one can imagine would carry two parallel posts, labelled respectively Head of Sales and Functional Head of Sales and, in this context it is impossible that anyone would have spent 3-5 years as 'functional', that is, 'acting' head of sales while the real holder of the post was for some reason *hors de combat*. But, if 'functional head of sales' means 'head of the sales department', why not say so and put everyone out of their misery?

G

Garden peas
Peas. Of 'garden', *The Dictionary of Diseased English* said, 'a meaningless word, beloved of the restaurant industry', and in six years that situation has changed not a scrap. Everywhere in the UK, on the middle level of eating places, this, that or the other dish will be 'served with chipped potatoes and baked beans or garden peas' (menu, Myllet Arms, Perivale, Middlesex, England, July 1982). It is worth considering if places which advertise 'garden peas' are not rendering themselves liable to prosecution under the Trade Descriptions Act, since the description is simply not true. The peas in question are certainly frozen and, equally certainly, they have been grown in a field, not a garden. A garden, as any competent lawyer would be able to demonstrate, is not a field, in the sense in which both words are commonly understood, and consequently an offence has been committed. The eating public is being misled tens of thousands of times every day and the motive for such deception is perfectly clear. 'Garden peas' suggests that the peas in question have been picked in a nearby garden, taken straight to the kitchen in a basket and shelled while the bloom is still on the pods. It is, alas, not so.

Gastronomic
Concerned with the art of good eating, with the cuisine of a particular country or region. One may therefore speak of 'gastronomic pleasures', 'gastronomic skills' or even refer to a particular meal or dish as 'a gastronomic disaster', but what exactly is 'a gastronomic menu'? If a restaurant advertises such a thing, the meaning is presumably that the menu is constructed with gastronomes in mind. In this case, 'a gastronomic menu, featuring dishes from the Great French Masters' (*The Birmingham Post*, 5 Nov 1981) should be viewed with some suspicion, not because good cooking is impossible in Birmingham, but because the proof of the cooking is in the eating, not in the menu. The menu may be admirable, but the reality may well not come up to it. If this should indeed prove to be the case, it is doubtful if the unfortunate customer

51

would have any redress in law. A 'gastronomic cuisine' would be quite another matter, however. Should it fail to produce dishes of which the Great French Masters would have approved, the restaurant could find itself in a most difficult legal situation, and quite rightly.

Genius

A person of exceptional ability, especially of a creative or inventive kind. Very few people in any generation qualify for the label. A true genius, if the word is to be used with reasonable care and precision, is a Mozart, a Newton, an Einstein. Consequently, it seems extremely unlikely that 'Wilber is truly a genius of our time' (*New York Review of Books*, 3 Dec 1981). This is without the slightest disrespect to Wilber who, as a novelist, may well be competent and readable above the average, but one is entitled to doubt if his skills or endowments place him in the Dickens or James Joyce class, which the word 'genius' would certainly suggest. If he indulges in this kind of exaggeration too often, the reviewer might find his public slipping away from him.

Gentleman

A person financially able to hire people to do his domestic work. In a Warwickshire village, therefore, 'a freehold detached gentleman's residence of character and charm' (*The Birmingham Post*, 5 Nov 1981) has to be understood roughly in this way. Some part of the house dates back to the 17th century and the whole property has been sensitively restored and well maintained. It has at least four and probably five bedrooms, two bathrooms and garaging for two cars. The garden is of a size which demands some paid help and the same is true of the house. No less can be expected of something officially labelled as 'a gentleman's residence', but the owner, unfortunately, will not necessarily be a gentleman.

Genuine

Unadulterated, being what it purports to be. But exactly what this may be is difficult to decide. A 'genuine' apple is clear enough, and so is a 'genuine' dog, but what is meant by 'Wolfschmidt Genuine Vodka' (*New Yorker*, 28 Sept 1981)? Etymologically, 'vodka' is one of the great Russian jokes, being a diminutive form of 'voda', 'water', and it could therefore be charmingly translated 'little water', which brings it into the same bracket as 'fire water'. In Russia, it is traditionally distilled from such everyday ingredients as rye and potatoes, together with such other sources of alcohol as may come readily to hand. What then is 'genuine vodka'? To qualify, does it simply have to be made with the usual Russian ingredients, with nothing else added or substituted? Is this what 'genuine' means? It is obviously not necessary for it to be Russian, since Wolfschmidt vodka is produced in the USA. Taking one thing with another, what the consumer is being told is that, in a world sadly full of shams and frauds, Wolfschmidt undertake to sell him something as close to Imperial Russian vodka as they can make it. But a blunt, honest statement like that would never sell anything, so 'genuine' it must be.

Gleaming

Polished and scrubbed until it shines? One does not know quite what to make of 'The gleaming Ramses Hilton' (Wings brochure, *Faraway Holidays*, Summer 1983). It happens to be white, but so are many other buildings in Cairo, so the reference can hardly be to its colour. On the other hand, it is unusually tall, so it might possibly 'gleam' because it catches more of the sun than its rivals. But, supposing this line of thought is misjudged, what remains? There is always the possibility that business would benefit if one intended 'gleaming' to imply that, whatever other hotels in Cairo might be like, the Hilton at least was spotless. Or perhaps the eyes of the staff are 'gleaming' at the thought of the tips they are going to receive, and shining eagerness has transferred itself to the hotel as a whole and caused it to gleam forth over the Nile and Egypt.

Good

Long. *See* BEST. 'Good' is a weather-forecaster's word, used with the approval of the British Broadcasting Corporation as a useful means of currying favour with the audience, simple-minded urban folk, for whom all sunshine is good and all rain bad. So one is told that 'the southern half of the country will have good sunny periods' (BBC Radio 4, 7.55 am, 16 July 1982). It should be noted that emotive words like 'good' and 'best', which apply value judgements to the weather, are never used in the weather-forecasts aimed at sailors and farmers, whose safety and prosperity demand facts, not sentiment.

Good taste

Desperate concern to do the right thing. People with good taste never mention it, people without it or on the verge of it are talking about it all the time, needing constant reassurance to set their minds at rest. For those with this good taste neurosis, there is no shortage of professional soothers, comforters, encouragers and flatterers. In the UK this is usually done in an indirect way, so that the vital ingredient of good taste is gently but unmistakably hinted at, but in the USA, where skins are thicker and where social position and the possession of money tend to be more obviously and publicly linked, plain statement is often the rule. The Pen and Pencil restaurant in New York, for example, will assure prospective customers that on these premises at least a meal will be 'served with particular care for your refined good taste' (*New Yorker*, 17 May 1982). This, to the cognoscenti, means that the lighting, cutlery, china and general ambiance will be of the middle-class American hostess type, known and approved in a thousand magazine advertisements and television commercials. The what, the food itself, is not of any very great importance, but the how is what the customers pay good money for. In the example quoted, 'taste' has, of course, absolutely nothing to do with the crude matter of eating, and it would be difficult to establish any real difference between 'good taste' and 'refined good taste'. To make completely sure of hitting the target, however, a double-barrelled shotgun is evidently advisable.

Gourmet

Applied to a restaurant or a meal, slightly above average. The word received a brief mention in *The Dictionary of Diseased English*, but the time has come to take more careful stock of it and, in particular, to enquire why it has such enormous potency and appeal in the USA and so little in the UK. Why does this American fashion stay so stubbornly at home?

The answer must surely lie in the difference between the average eating-place in the USA and in the UK. It is fair to say that the business of nourishing oneself outside one's home is, in general, accomplished more hygienically but more crudely or boringly in the USA. If the base line is a hamburger or a steak, then one does not have to rise very far above it to reach the 'gourmet' level and it becomes possible to sing the praises of 'hundreds of gourmet restaurants in a wide price range' (advert by Broward County Tourist Development Council for holidays in South Florida, *Sunday Telegraph*, 20 Dec 1981). One may fairly doubt, however, if any of these 'hundreds of gourmet restaurants' would receive even the smallest accolade from the *Guide Michelin* inspectors. In the USA, with luck — and one needs the luck — 'gourmet' means 'eatable'.

Graciously

In an advertiser's version of upper middle-class style. *The Dictionary of Diseased English* has 'gracious' and 'graciousness', but not 'graciously'.

The adverb has become much more common during the past five years, especially in the USA, where 'gracious' and its derivatives are at a premium. It is possible in the USA for a restaurant to inform the well-bred world that it provides 'delicious meals served graciously' (*New York Times*, 27 Sept 1981) without risking a smile or worse, but the same expression in the UK might well provoke mirth, especially among the young and irreverent. On this side of the Atlantic, there are many who yearn for graciousness and who do their humble best to contrive it, but who could never bring themselves to utter the word. The Americans have no such inhibitions, and it is not impossible, with the steady grading-up of social ambitions and expectations, that we, in the UK, will go the same way. We have, after all, had the dreadful 'gracious living' with us for a long time, to manure the ground, and it seems, if anything, to be found more frequently now than five years ago, when there were welcome signs that it was being killed off by ridicule. But there is obviously a real psychological need for it and it has survived — 'Harrods simply cuts the cost of gracious living' (*Sunday Telegraph*, 2 Jan 1983).

Grand
Classic, traditional. Anything can be graded up by putting 'grand' in front of it. The trick is an old one, even with food and wine — Grand Marnier, for instance — but its use in conjunction with American food is daring, to say the least. One finds, for instance, a restaurant which commends itself to public attention as 'featuring the best of the Grand American Cuisine' (*New Yorker*, 17 May 1982). On closer inspection, the Grand American Cuisine turns out to consist of Prime Steak, Swordfish, Lamb Chops and Salmon, a somewhat odd quartet, difficult to place in any tradition at all. But 'Grand' nips all criticism and doubt in the bud.

Grass roots
Where nothing grew before, wild. This expression has acquired so many shades of meaning during the ten years or so of its existence as a piece of management jargon that it has lost whatever precision and usefulness it may once have had. With 'grass roots opinion' one knew where one was. This was the way in which simple people looked at the world and politics, thinking rooted in practical experience. But what is the point of 'grass roots', when an engineer is told that he will be 'responsible for the start up and commissioning of a grass roots refinery based on the Saudi Arabian cost' (*The Daily Telegraph*, 5 Nov 1981)? This is nothing more than a new refinery, acres of pipework where there was nothing but sand

before. And what sense is one to make of a company's promise that a man will be moved onwards and upwards to higher things 'after 2 years grass roots selling experience' (*The Daily Telegraph*, 10 Dec 1981)? Is this selling experience in previously virgin territory, the first selling experience of a young man's career, experience of selling goods to peasants, or what? It is easier to guess what a company has in mind when it refers to a person's 'skill as an operator at top level and grass roots' (*The Daily Telegraph*, 18 Feb 1982). Ten years ago this would have been 'able to communicate at senior management and shop floor level'. Whether 'grass roots' is considered more democratic and friendly by the grass roots people themselves is difficult to say, but it probably causes less prickliness and insurrection than 'bottom' would.

Gratification
Pleasure, satisfaction. A word much in vogue among social scientists, whose livelihood depends on their talent for avoiding simple statements. It sits well in such nonsense sentences as 'The findings indicate that the major effects of the size of winnings are an increase in gratification acceptance and a decrease in future attainable orientations' (*American Sociological Review*, xiv, no. 1, Feb 1980), a suggested translation of which is 'The more you win, the happier you are and the less likely to worry about the future', a sound observation on human nature, which deserved not to be buried alive under such a thick wad of verbal cottonwool.

Great
Pleasant, impressive. 'Great' is a piece of American pomposity which is wheeled in so frequently and on such a variety of occasions that it has lost practically all meaning. Eminent people are under a social obligation to reply 'Great, just great', when asked how they are feeling the day after having had half their intestines removed, and a manufacturer of reproduction furniture can assure us that 'Great rooms are created by but a few pieces of uncommon elegance' (advert by John Widdicomb, *New Yorker*, 15 June 1980). With the currency so debased, there seems little point in arguing about the last occasion on which the USA had a great President. The word would benefit from a long, long rest, but it seems unlikely to get one.

Green fields
Where competition does not yet exist, where the market is only now beginning to develop. Still fairly new and fresh, this piece of businessese

has all the signs of becoming exceedingly tedious during the next year or two. It has pioneer-life overtones and this nearly always means that industrial people, who are great romantics, will flock to it, their hearts beating faster at the thought of 'these green fields opportunities within one of Asia's most dynamic economies' (*The Daily Telegraph*, 18 Feb 1982).

Groundbreaking
First, elementary, pioneering. The word is now in official use among literary critics who, at the slightest opportunity, are liable to praise a book for being 'a groundbreaking introduction' to this or that (*New York Review of Books*, 3 Dec 1981). The reader may well be left in some doubt as to the critic's meaning, however. In the example just given, for instance, is 'groundbreaking' to be interpreted as 'breaking new ground', that is, 'pioneering', or as 'opening up the subject', that is, 'elementary'? One could very easily find oneself buying the wrong book and cursing the critic, instead of thanking him.

Grown-up
For sharp, wideawake adults. This can be a difficult one. Consider, for example, 'a casino full of grown-up games' (*New Yorker*, 14 June 1982). Does this mean 'games for grown-ups', and, if so, what exactly are they? Or is it 'sophisticated, refined, highly developed games'? Let us suppose that the first choice is correct. Is baccarat a 'grown-up game', or is the casino full of games which are in some way more grown-up than baccarat, games demanding great intelligence and experience and a high degree of self-protection and cunning? What, if this guess is right, are the names of these unspecified games? If ADULT means 'pornographic' — and 'grown-up' is, after all, a synonym of 'adult' — can it be that the casino is full of pornographic games? Only a personal visit to the establishment is likely to clear the matter up.

H

Handcrafted

Made by hand. *See* CRAFTED. One is either in tune with 'craft', 'crafted' and 'handcrafted' or one is not. They are masonic words, making life worthwhile for the initiates and causing those outside the cult to boil and gnash their teeth. There is no half-way position, and no real point in trying either to attack or define words which are essentially magical. Believers require no explanations and unbelievers can search all day for meaning and find none. But conscience and a sense of public duty demand that the attempt should be made, if society is to have any rational basis at all.

The difference between 'handcrafted' and 'crafted' on the one hand and 'handmade' on the other is entirely one of intention. To say that a chair or suit or a pork pie is 'handmade' is a plain statement of fact; to say that it is 'crafted' or 'handcrafted' is to introduce an emotional element into the situation — 'It's really *hand*crafted) Isn't that *wonderful*! Not a machine near it! In these days! My, my, that really is worth paying all that moncy for! *Hand*craftcd! Think of that!' 'Handmade' allows the listener or reader to remain sober; 'handcrafted' should leave him swaying slightly on his fcct, moaning and sighing, and with his eyes closed, with all power of judgement gone. 'The original watch, handcrafted from an authentic $20 gold piece' (*Swissair Gazette*, Oct 1981) gets buyers where it wants them.

Hands-on

The great international management mystery phrase, with no inside agreement as to what it means. *The Dictionary of Diseased English* reported three suggestions from people confident of having the right answer — 'in daily contact with the most important issues; concerned with practical matters, not theory; responsible for policy making'. Since 'hands-on' is used even more intensively today than it was five years ago, some central meaning should have begun to reveal itself by now, but this does not, alas, seem to be the case. One is encouraged to feel that 'hands-

59

on' may possibly be a synonym for 'first-class' or 'top quality'. Either would make a perfectly good alternative in either 'Hands-on hospital controller wanted for small psychiatric hospital in Connecticut' (*New York Times*, 27 Sept 1981), or 'The position is for a hands-on professional' (*Boston Globe*, 11 Oct 1981). But so, too, would 'red-haired', 'flat-footed' or 'graduate'.

Health care

The care of people who are ill. *The Dictionary of Diseased English* was concerned mainly with the 'health care industry', but noted in passing that 'a high proportion of 'health care', that is, the work with which doctors are concerned, is related to ill-health care'. One could put this another way by saying that if there were more health care there would be less health care. Within the medical profession itself, especially in the USA, 'health care' increasingly means medical and surgical treatment, rather than what it should be, persuading people to follow a way of life which makes them less likely to fall ill and have accidents. But, unless it is devised with extreme cunning, in the form of expensive 'check-ups', encouraging people to look after their own health is not good, either for doctors' pockets or for the pharmaceutical industry. Much trouble and ingenuity is therefore taken to keep 'health care' closely meshed in with hospitals and clinics, a process well illustrated by a reference to 'a progressive teaching hospital designed to providing (*sic*) optimum health care to the community (*New York Times*, 27 Sept 1981). 'Optimum health care' should certainly be the aim of any civilized society, but 'excellent hospital conditions', which is what is meant here, is something very different.

Health food

Food for human consumption bought from a health food shop, such as 'Health Foods, Bristol, Ltd.' (*Yellow Pages* telephone directory, 1982). *See also* REAL FOOD, NATURAL FOOD, and WHOLE. All foods which are not actually poisonous are 'health foods', in the sense that, sensibly cooked and eaten in moderation and reasonable variety, they help to maintain the body in health. But 'health food' shops have their own special definition of the term. A careful look at their windows and shelves will show that they are concerned only with vegetarian foodstuffs. They do not sell meat, fish, eggs or dairy produce, the implication clearly being that such food is unhealthy. Since, however, 'health food' sounds much better than 'vegetarian food', 'health food' it has to be.

One further point should be mentioned, as a guide through what has become a rather baffling food maze. Whereas all Real Food shops, Whole Food shops and Natural Food shops would claim to be, in their own different ways, Health Food shops, the reverse is not necessarily true. It is perfectly possible for what we will call for convenience RF, WF and NF shops to sell certain commodities, such as eggs, butter and cheese, which HF shops would take care to exclude. Equally, HF shops do not always emphasize that what they have on sale is always grown without the aid of artificial fertilizers and chemical pesticides. To a confirmed eater of forbidden foods, the RF, WF, NF AND HF situation must seem as strange and confusing as the multiplicity of Christian sects does to a Moslem.

Heap
An inchoate pile, an unorganized mass. A heap of food of any kind does not, to the discriminating eater, sound very appealing, yet the proprietors of restaurants on both sides of the Atlantic are showing considerable affection for the term, believing, probably rightly, that a great many people are not discriminating at all and are quite as likely to be attracted by quantity as by quality. So one is offered, for example, 'a heap of freshly baked pork ribs' (Tennessee Pancake House, Leicester Square, London, July 1982). But, if one is thinking about value for money, or even sheer bulk, how many pork ribs go to the heap? Or about how many? Two? Four? Six? It could make a difference. With the now old-fashioned 'two pork chops', one knew where one was, but a 'heap' of the things is a pretty vague concept and one has an uneasy suspicion that the vagueness may not be altogether accidental.

Hearty
Heavy, bulky, meaty. 'Hearty appetites', 'hearty eaters', and 'hearty meals' have been with us for generations and we have a reasonably clear idea of what they mean. As an addition to the family, we now have 'hearty dishes', and this seems to deserve a little analysis. A 'hearty dish' is always a meat dish, as is made clear by "Eye of the Swan' may be served chilled with chicken or fish, yet has enough body to complement heartier dishes' (*New Yorker*, 14 June 1982). One could, of course, make a very hearty meal indeed off chicken or fish, but in a country with such a strongly emphasized and highly valued meat culture as the USA has, a meal of this type would hardly count.

High flyer, high flier
Super-ambitious person, someone earmarked for early promotion. These often rather irritating people, prodigies who are good and know it, future managing directors and prime ministers at the age of six, have always been with us, although, to judge by the frequency with which the moern term 'high flyer' is used, they must be in more plentiful supply nowadays than they were 50 or 100 years ago. Some organizations, indeed, give the impression of only recruiting young men who have a field-marshal's baton in their knapsack and, with every employee a high flyer, the atmosphere must get more than a little tense at time. There are, however, good reasons for feeling that 'high flyer' has now, after 20 years of fevered overuse, descended into the cliché class, with nobody giving much thought to what it means. How else can one account for such absurdities as 'applicants must be self-motivated high flyers' (*The Daily Telegraph*, 1 July 1982), which is a description of aeroplanes, not people? Such a sentence does, however, provide additional evidence, should any be needed, of the business world's remarkable lack of ability to see anything funny about its habits and attitudes.

High-level
Big. No business concern with any pretensions to respectability could bring itself to refer publicly to 'big customers' or 'big accounts'. Some such alternative as 'major', 'substantial' or 'important' always has to be found, so that size is always equated with quality. 'High-level' has become another great favourite in recent years. It is a most valuable tool for keeping sentences floating well above the ground. 'Individual responsibilities will include maintenance and servicing of current high-level accounts' (*The Daily Telegraph*, 17 Dec 1981) is a fair example, although here one has the added complication of trying to decide what difference, if any, there might be between 'a current high-level account' and 'a high-level current account'.

Highly acclaimed
With a good reputation, well thought of. But the problem is the same as with that other much-used confidence trick, AWARD–WINNING. By whom is whatever it is 'highly acclaimed'? Until one knows this, the value of the acclaim cannot be assessed. So the company which is, one is told, 'a highly acclaimed subsidiary of Capper Neill p.l.c.' (*The Daily Telegraph*, 24 June 1982) may well be brilliantly managed and magnificently successful, the toast of investors, brokers and stock exchanges the world over, but, equally, it may be 'highly acclaimed' only by itself and

by Capper Neill p.l.c. One can hardly be blamed for having one's suspicions. And so, too, with 'the highly-acclaimed radio version of J.R.R. Tolkien's *Lord of the Rings* (BBC Radio 4, 17 July 1982). From whom has all the applause been coming? One would so much like to know.

High visibility
Being noticed in all the right places and by all the right people. In any organization, most of the people employed are allowed no visibility at all. They are kept well away from the front of the stage, beavering away at what they are paid to do and with no great hopes of moving upward or indeed anywhere. To be 'high visibility' is consequently to be immensely privileged. Such a person may even be permitted to sign his own letters with his own name, so that his visibility is carried far and wide by the Post Office. He will be at least a major in the industrial army, occupying 'a key management role, with professional high visibility and opportunities for rapid advancement' (*New York Times*, 27 Sept 1981). In this case, it is the holder of the job who has 'high visibility', but at other times it is the job itself, as in 'this high-visibility post' (*Boston Globe*, 11 Oct 1981).

The image is a curious one, suggesting perhaps soldiers crawling over the ground on their bellies to avoid being noticed and shot, while their gallant leaders rush forward upright, heedless of danger and with a good chance of a medal at the end of it all. Or a speaker at a May Day rally in Trafalgar Square, standing on the podium for all to see and heckle. In industry and commerce, as in the army, to possess 'high visibility' can be uncomfortable and even dangerous, which is no doubt why most people would prefer to go through life on their bellies.

Hospitality
Welcome, tourism. 'Hospitality' is a shockingly abused word and it is not difficult to nail the villains responsible. The essence of hospitality is that it shall be given freely, willingly and with a warm heart. To invite friends to dinner or for the weekend and then to present them with a bill on departure would quite rightly be considered scandalous behaviour and, once the word got round, one would find oneself seriously short of friends. But the hotel and tourist industries, in effect, do exactly this. A hotel will speak of its 'guests', as if they are being fed and lodged free, and an Australian hotel goes so far as to announce that it is 'a famous name in the hospitality industry' (brochure of the Wentworth Hotel, Sydney, 1982), which it most certainly is not. It is a famous name in the hotel industry, and let a spade be called a spade.

'Hospitality' has been so downgraded by commercial interests that it has come to mean, at its best, little more than 'friendliness'. When a tourist board in the USA looks around its region and publicizes 'the hospitality of the people' (*Arkansas, the Natural State*, the Arkansas Department of Parks and Tourism, 1982), it does not mean, alas, that the inhabitants of Arkansas are renowned for their kindness in taking strangers into their homes and offering them free meals and a bed for the night. It means that, by and large, they are friendly and unlikely to loose fierce dogs at passers-by or to open fire on them. But, with only the word of the Department of Tourism to go by, a literal-minded person could be pardoned for believing that a visit to Arkansas was going to cost him very little.

I

Idyllic
Charming, picturesque. There is no British Standard by which to measure the idyllic and consequently the quality and extent of any particular idyll must be largely in the eye of the beholder. It all depends on what kind of surroundings one is used to. To anyone forced to spend most of his time in an urban slum, Kew Gardens or Croxteth Park, Liverpool, would seem idyllic, but to a person reared in mid-Devon or the Scottish Highlands, such places could well seem something of a let-down and 'idyllic' would be much too flattering a description. It is clearly a word to be approached with great caution and a translation of 'Our Head Office and factory are situated in an idyllic situation in South Wales' (*The Daily Telegraph*, 4 Feb 1982) could be decidedly tricky. A photograph would undoubtedly help.

Immaculate
Faultlessly maintained. *The Dictionary of Diseased English* made a brief mention of this piece of house agentry and suggested that a realistic definition might be, 'not in immediate need of redecoration'. This translation seems as likely as any. The conventional meaning of the word is 'spotless, without blemish', but even the most enthusiastic of estate agents would hardly be likely to claim this of one of the properties on his books. What kind of house, then, is 'an immaculate Mediterranean split level villa' (*Country Life*, 21 May 1981)? Does it have absolutely no bird droppings on the window sills, no scratch on the paintwork, and not a single cracked tile in the bathroom or stain on the parquet? This would be most unlikely to correspond to the facts. All that is probably meant is that the house has been recently painted and that the garden is tidy.

The word has been worked very hard for a number of years and there are unmistakable signs that it is no longer the power it once was. One now finds it reinforced by an adverb, something which never happened two or three years ago, when for a house to be spotless was regarded as being as close to perfection as one was likely to get. Those days have evidently passed, since today it is possible to be offered an 'utterly immaculate ground-floor flat in this award-winning block' (advertisement by Faron Sutaria, *London Property*, mid-Jan 1983).

Impact
Sales, market share. 'In the field of plain paper copiers, the impact made by Canon is exceeding all expectations' (*The Daily Telegraph*, 17 Sept 1981) illustrates the understandable wish of commercial firms to have an impact, a satisfyingly aggressive word, but it also provides an example of the extent to which business lets itself down time and time again by having no sense of the ridiculous. A firm called Canon simply should not tell the world about its impact. 'The share of the market obtained by Canon' would have been much safer, although it would have lacked the hitting image so esteemed by marketing men.

Importantly
Important. The arrival of 'importantly' in the UK from the USA ten years or so ago was regrettable, marking as it did the spread of the belief that, if three syllables were good, four must be even better. 'More importantly, the interaction between terminal location and distance cues ... ' (*The British Journal of Psychiatry*, 77.81) started a paragraph, thereby showing how professional, modern and scientific it was, far superior to the deadbeats who continued to say 'More important', in the way their fathers and grandfathers had done. But there is no need to be taken in by such crude tricks. All that 'more importantly' proves is that the author keeps bad company, reads a lot of scientific papers and would emigrate to the USA if he had half a chance.

Impressive
Large, pleasing. This has become a much-favoured word with the new generation of estate agents. It is used in such contexts as 'late 18th century country residence of impressive proportions' (*Country Life*, 21 May 1981) and, without seeing the property in question, it is impossible to decide what it means. One possibility is simply to translate 'of impressive proportions' as 'large', so that a prospective purchaser finds himself confronted with nothing more complicated than a large country house. On the other hand, if it is an 18th century building, the proportions might well be impressive, since one is concerned with a period when architects knew what they were about. Estate agents being what they are, the first guess seems more likely to be right.

Incumbent
Person holding, appointment to, applicant for a post. Until the 1970s, 'incumbent' referred almost always to a clergyman. One was the 'incumbent' of a living or a parish, and of nothing else, except jokingly. It was, for example, possible to refer to 'an incumbent' of Dartmoor or Wormwood Scrubs. The business world then decided to make a take-over bid for the word, in order, one presumes, to make very ordinary activities sound much more grand than they really were. This practice has become much more widespread in recent years, often with laughable results. A firm requiring a Business Gifts Sales Manager, a position with, one might have thought, a remarkably low spiritual content, will speak of 'the successful incumbent ...' (*The Daily Telegraph*, 17 Sept 1981) and, to those who remember the word before corruption and degradation set in, 'Incumbents will develop designs for 800 kV substations' (*The Daily Telegraph*, 15 June 1981) may well conjure up a picture of a drawing office full of gentlemen in clerical collars, while 'The incumbent will work closely with sales management' (*The Daily Telegraph*, 17 Sept 1981) has a strong suggestion of an industrial chaplain about it.

In-depth
Considerably, not superficial, profound, thorough. A business catch-phrase for the past ten years, 'in-depth' is at last showing strong signs of having exhausted itself and of entering the first stages of senility. Unconscious funnies containing the expression are becoming more numerous, sure evidence that it has now become a cliché with very little real meaning at all. One could instance, 'If you are a professional Reservoir or Drilling Engineer and have in-depth experience and an honours degree' (*The Sunday Times*, 25 Nov 1981), where the thought of being required to follow the drill bit to the bottom of a deep hole might be frightening to some. There are bound to be those holidaymakers, too, who would not be greatly attracted by 'escorted tours that include in-depth sightseeing' (*New Yorker*, 17 May 1982), while 'You must therefore have an in-depth knowledge of the garment industry' (*The Daily Telegraph*, 12 Jan 1982) has remarkable possibilities. There are good reasons now for committing the body of 'in-depth' to the deep.

Indirect
None at all. This is a very fine new estate agency creation indeed, a little masterpiece worthy of the textbooks. It is to be found in such contexts as 'prestigeous (*sic*) Tudor-style house, with indirect frontage to the River Thames' (*The Times*, 4 Nov 1981). A little reflection will soon show that

either a house has a frontage to the river or it does not. What, then, is 'indirect frontage' supposed to mean? It means, in fact, that someone else's property comes between yours and the river, which is another way of saying that yours has no frontage at all. It is true that, if you should happen to have friendly neighbours, they might be willing to let you sit on their riverside lawn from time to time, and that you would not have to walk very far in order to get there, but that is hardly the same as being able to moor a boat and dangle your toes in the water at the edge of your very own riverside frontage. It is not unlike advertising the Strand as having 'an indirect frontage to the Thames'. It would have, of course, if only Somerset House, Aldwych and all those other damned buildings weren't in the way.

Individual
Unlike any other. Few people enjoy being indistinguishable from the herd and houses presumably feel the same way. In order to protect oneself as a prospective buyer, it is, however, necessary to subject house agents' descriptions like 'a superbly managed individual property of manageable proportions' (*Country Life*, 21 May 1981) to fairly severe analysis. 'Individual' is unfortunately no guarantee of beauty, comfort, or indeed pleasantness of any kind and, no matter how superbly managed it may be or how manageable its proportions, it may still be utterly hideous and appallingly inconvenient to live in. 'Individual' is often, perhaps usually, an adjective of the last resort, employed when a place has made even an estate agent turn pale and when no other word seems sufficiently cosmetic.

Infinite
Limitless, subject to no bounds of space or time. The English language has few stronger words and common sense would suggest that one would be wise to use it sparingly. The advertising men, brave fellows that they are, are not daunted. They are, for instance, perfectly willing to tell us that a hotel is 'conveniently situated for infinite shopping and sightseeing' (*New Yorker*, 14 Sept 1981). Some of the weaker ones among us might possibly feel that the prospect of 'infinite' shopping or 'infinite' sightseeing is too terrifying to contemplate, a life sentence to which no human being should be condemned. Perhaps, however, 'infinite' means 'infinitely good', so that it is a quality, not a quantity term. That may seem a trifle exaggerated but, in the kind of world where grand hotels and their clients operate, it is a possible interpretation. More cynical readers are likely to believe that in such a context as this,

'infinite' is simply a synonym for 'wonderful', or equally possibly, that it means absolutely nothing at all, and that 'infinite shopping and sightseeing' is nothing more than 'shopping and sightseeing'. But that, to someone who is paying 150 dollars a night for the room, would almost amount to saying that one had been swindled. If one has paid an infinite price, one surely deserves an infinite reward.

Innovative

Keen to introduce new ideas, not hidebound. In today's management world, 'innovative' is fairly close to being the opposite of 'conservative', but it has become so grossly overused that one often wonders if it really carries much meaning at all. If everyone is supposed, as a matter of course, to be passionately addicted to progress, new systems and new techniques, what is the point of perpetually labouring the point? Does it actually make the slightest difference to the list of applicants, or to the final result, if an organization says that it wants 'an innovative individual with substantial experience in long-range planning' (*New York Times*, 27 Sept 1981)? Does this sift out the non-innovative types in advance? Or is the situation similar to what was normal in Victorian times, when everyone who wanted to become a member of parliament or a headmaster took care to be a Christian? With the labour market as it is, would anyone with the slightest ambition be so foolish as to admit that he was not innovative?

Insight

Informed knowledge. This usually highly flattering American term has entered the British bloodstream, but it is just possible, given vigilance and skilful treatment, that the spread of the poison may be arrested in time. 'Insight' is a useful word, worth preserving against corruption. Properly used, it means 'ability to see in the heart of a problem, understanding of what a situation really is or why a person acts as he does'. This is not at all what is implied by 'rounding out your insight to this historic part of the world' (*New Yorker*, 19 Oct 1981). If one tries to squeeze some sense out of this, the result would be something like 'learning something about the history of this part of the world'. That tourists will acquire 'insight' into the problems of Italy or Ireland as a consequence of a holiday visit is lacking in reality, but it sounds good and gives a nice serious-minded gloss to one's vacation.

Insightful

Sensitive, skilled in interpeting human behaviour. This truly dreadful word is frighteningly popular among American publishers and reviewers. Each year brings a larger crop of such monstrosities as 'We periodically publish papers by insightful authors' (mailing by Baywood Publishing Company, Farmingdale, New York, 1981), and 'A marvellously good book, insightful and revealing' (*New York Review of Books*, 3 Dec 1981). The rot has gone so deep that it is almost impossible to imagine a novel or a biography which is not 'insightful'. No self-respecting publishing house would have it on its list, no author with a living to earn would admit to have been responsible for such an un-American thing. It is a pleasure to be able to report that, as yet, the adjective is mercifully rare in the UK.

Inspirational

Leading one towards higher things. The word suggests the more unpleasant aspects of religion in the USA, sticky with sentiment, Rotary on its knees. 'Inspired' and its derivatives have been so debased by promotionism and religiosity that it is almost impossible to use them any more. Anything described as 'inspirational' one would do very well to avoid. One can only hope that 'Readers will find here a richly inspirational novel' (*New York Review of Books*, 3 Dec 1981) is intended as a warning, but there are no doubt those who would consider it a recommendation.

Interface

Relations, co-operation, discussion. 'Interface' is a cartoonist's dream. Few of today's management words have such ludicrous possibilities but, as we have remarked elsewhere in the present *Dictionary*, management and its acolytes are not exactly famous for their sense of humour. An Interface Anthology, suitably illustrated, is an attractive publishing idea. In preparation for it, one can offer a few particularly choice recent examples. A salesman is required 'with demonstrated ability in client interface' (*The Daily Telegraph*, 21 Jan 1982). This has intriguing possibilities. Does the salesman have to produce photographs of himself looking at a customer straight in the eyeballs? Or hypnotizing his victim? Or giving him the kiss of life? 'There will be a substantial interface with project engineers' (*The Daily Telegraph*, 15 Dec 1981) suggests a degree of intimacy which not all project engineers would find pleasing, and there might well be candidates who would decide to look elsewhere after being told that 'you'll be interfacing with all levels of management' (*New York Times*, 27 Sept 1981).

In modern business one must clearly be prepared to suppress one's personal feelings and inhibitions in the interests of the cause, just as today's footballers have to accept being publicly cuddled by the rest of the team after scoring a goal. The range of people with whom one might be expected to interface seems limitless. One company wants 'an experienced Senior Estimator to interface with clients and other engineering disciplines within the Company' (*The Daily Telegraph*, 4 Feb 1982) — how exactly does one interface with a discipline? — and another says that 'Personal qualities are of paramount importance for effective internal interfacing with engineering, sales and contract management and customers' (*The Daily Telegraph*, 21 Oct 1981). 'Internal interfacing' suggests not only the remarkable 'personal qualities' which are demanded for the post, but an unusual kind of anatomy and the ability to withstand pain, since 'interfacing with engineering' does not sound at all comfortable. It is probably safer and more agreeable if departments are encouraged to interface directly with one another, with no people involved. This seems to be what is meant by the company which refers to 'the interface between the UK legal department, the sales force and a variety of external organisations' (*The Daily Telegraph*, 17 Sept 1981).

But, beyond doubt, the prize for the finest piece of managerial nonsense of its year has to go to the American concern which told ambitious young men that 'candidates must have the hands-on ability to troubleshoot the software interface' (*Boston Globe*, 11 Oct 1981). This is *hors concours*.

Interpersonal

As between one person and another. There are quite a number of interpersonal skills, not all of them publishable, and one wonders exactly which ones the company had in mind when it told prospective members of its staff that 'considerable interpersonal skills are required (*The Sunday Times*, 25 Oct 1981). Are 'interpersonal skills' substantially different from what used to be called 'man-management'? Are they perhaps the same as those involved in 'handling people'? Or is one to understand something of quite another order, perhaps 'conversation', or 'flattery', or 'calming down'? Or possibly 'persuading to reveal secrets'? The phrase is far from satisfactory. It has overtones of fencing, of battles of wits, of sharp exchanges between equals, but one cannot be sure if this is what is really intended.

Involvement

Employment, co-operation, interest, slavery. For an organization to tell members of its staff that they must regard themselves as having been bought body and soul for 24 hours a day and 7 days a week would probably not be good for its image. It is possible, nevertheless, to speak of 'total involvement', which means exactly the same thing, and to get away with it. Recently, however, the scope of the word appears to have broadened considerably, so much so that the reader is likely to find himself somewhat bemused. 'Visit a Ford or Lincoln-Mercury dealer and take a close look at what total employee, management, union and supplier involvement can involve' (*New Yorker*, 17 May 1982), the Ford Motor Company tells the world. This certainly sounds impressive, but what in fact does it mean, if anything? What Ford probably intends to convey is that the people who make and sell Ford cars are doing their best to make and sell reliable cars. At least, one hopes this is what lies behind the sentence. The thought of anyone being 'totally involved' in producing and marketing motor vehicles is too horrible to contemplate. Surely God did not create man for such an appalling destiny?

But perhaps even worse is the career which has included, as an essential part of a candidate's experience, 'previous involvement with the paint industry' (*The Daily Telegraph*, 11 Dec 1981). How, one wonders, is the unfortunate man ever going to get the stuff off himself and his clothes and make himself presentable again?

J

Jack-booted
Brutal, tyrannical, fascist. When the Communist press refers to 'that other jack-booted idol of the Tory Party Conference, Michael Heseltine' (*Morning Star*, 5 Nov 1981), it does not really expect its readers to believe that Mr Heseltine dresses and behaves like a member of Hitler's S.S. The political Left, however, has its own special brand of insults inherited from the grand days of the 1930s, when Fascism and Nazism represented all that was evil and when virtue was in Russian keeping. Its logic since then has been interesting, if a little over-simplified. In Mr Heseltine's case, it runs roughly as follows. Hitler was supported by the political Right, Mr Heseltine belongs to the political Right, therefore Mr Heseltine is a Fascist and indistinguishable from Hitler and Mussolini, even to the extent of wearing jackboots secretly under his trousers. Observations suggests, however, that 'jack-booted' does not form part of the daily vocabulary of the average British worker and that only in very rare instances would he have the faintest idea of the meaning of the word. This, however, is probably beside the point. By employing such words issue after issue, the *Morning Star* is carrying out a series of religious exercises which amount to bowing in the direction of Moscow at least once a day.

K

Knuckle down
To apply oneself. The phrase is an old one and, in its right place, there is absolutely no objection to it. For a boy to 'knuckle down' to his mathematics is entirely fit and proper. The meaning is clear and the sentiment admirable. What the business world has made of 'knuckle down' is another matter altogether. In their desperate and never-ending search for words which will describe the self-sacrifice and unremitting toil of our managerial heroes, industrial spokesmen are all too likely to resort to such fearsome outpourings as 'the ability of the candidate to knuckle down himself or herself to the nitty-gritty of spin-off planning and development' (*The Sunday Times*, 25 Jan 1981). Knuckling down to the nitty-gritty sounds painful and a few hours of it would probably be sufficient to prove one's moral worth. What is particularly nasty and hypocritical about sentences such as this is the way in which everyday expressions are woven into the jargon, as evidence of the firm's down-to-earth democracy and essential friendliness. No-one should be taken in by such transparent ruses. Colloquialisms are no proof whatever of a warm, honest, kindly working atmosphere. All this use of 'knuckle down', 'nitty-gritty' and the rest is bogus. How bogus one can quickly realize, by observing that the person responsible for the masterpiece quoted above was apparently not aware that one does not 'knuckle oneself down' to something, one 'knuckles down'. And 'knuckling down' to 'the nitty-gritty' shows that no thought at all had been given to the meaning of these expressions. They were simply strung together like beads or sausages.

L

Lady

Woman. This is an extraordinarily difficult word for a foreigner to use correctly, and many true-born Englishmen and Englishwomen display a far from sure touch where it is concerned. The main difficulty is that the further down the social scale one goes, the more strongly women object to being called women. Educated women prefer it, uneducated women resent it. There are, however, one or two subtleties and complications which have to be observed. In the uniformed services, women are always women. 'Police ladies' would be as unthinkable as the Ladies Royal Army Corps. And then, at the upper end of British society, women might be women to one another, but they might well expect to be referred to as 'ladies' by their own kind of men. At work, it may be 'women staff' or 'female staff', but never 'ladies staff' or 'lady staff'. The problem used to be dreadfully complicated with lavatories, since no matter whether one labelled them 'Ladies' or 'Women', somebody was bound to be annoyed. The problem has been solved by using a symbol, which can be interpreted, according to choice, as either 'ladies' or 'women'.

So sensitive are working-class feelings in this matter and so anxious are employers to avoid strikes, trouble and deputations that 'tea lady', 'cleaning lady' and 'canteen lady' are the rule. Once pride is satisfied and dignity safeguarded by the use of 'lady', tea can be prepared, offices cleaned and canteens operated in the usual way. So one finds 'Mrs Pamela Ozarak, a Wokingham tea lady' (*The Times*, 29 Oct 1982) as a matter of course, although in this particular example there may be more than a touch of the patronizing. One cannot feel that all this class-consciousness is healthy and it can certainly be perilous for those who are not bred and trained to it.

Leading-edge

Vanguard, ahead of the rest, the latest. The metaphor, beloved of industrial people, comes from aeronautics, where the front edge of an aircraft wing is the leading edge. A person, object or process which is 'leading-edge' is therefore in the forefront of progress, likely to have considerable influence on future developments. It is possible to refer with admiration to 'a young company involved in exciting leading-edge technology' (*Boston Globe*, 11 Oct 1981). In such a context as this, 'leading-edge' means nothing more than 'new', but the extra connotations of sharpness and cutting make the term specially attractive. A new technology is one thing, but a technology which slices its way through the ageing present and towards a wonderful future, pushing aside everything in its path, is much more likely to capture the imagination. Unfortunately, however, the reality does not always match up to the expectations aroused by such a fine expression. One may, to put the matter bluntly, find oneself the victim of a skilful confidence trick, led along by the leading edge, so to speak.

Lifestyle
Public image, social bric-à-brac, way of living. There is an important difference between the old word, 'style', and the new one, 'lifestyle'. 'Style' is concerned with personality, with the way one presents oneself to the world. 'Lifestyle', on the other hand, relates much more to the trappings of a person's life, to methods and choices of spending money. The advertisers and the colour supplements know all about 'lifestyle' and spend much of their time making this or that 'lifestyle' appear attractive and desirable. Cars, houses, holidays, clothes and furniture have a great deal to do with 'lifestyle'. A naked savage living in a reed hut can have 'style', but his 'lifestyle' would have no interest for the advertisers, because it does not involve spending money. He would be allowed 'a way of life', but not a 'lifestyle', except possibly by social anthropologists. 'Lifestyle', in other words, is essentially synthetic. It can be prescribed, bought, and changed at will. It can be said of a range of wallpapers and furnishing fabrics, for example, that 'they encompass your whole life style' (*New York Times*, 27 Sept 1981) and of a house or flat that it provides 'a totally different lifestyle for people who want a second home with none of the problems of the first' (*Boston Globe*, 11 Oct 1981). There are, inevitably, lifestyle consultants, just as there are psychiatrists and financial advisers. Such experts will, for a suitable fee, provide 'a discussion of your lifestyle and design problems' (*New York Times*, 27 Sept 1981). Lifestyle problems, marriage problems, money problems, they are all evidence that one has accepted one's duties as a citizen and consumer.

One's lifestyle certainly needs all the care and attention one can give it. Its influence is everywhere and in everything. One has thoughts of trying a new keeps-you-fit foodstuff and one is told by the manufacturers that 'It's only fair to the product that you rebalance your lifestyle' (*London Portrait*, Jan 1983), at which the lifestyle would surely be entitled to ask who was tail and who was dog.

Life support
Sustaining life, making life physically or mentally more tolerable and comfortable. If one wants one's speech and writing to retain any precision at all, this dreadful expression should certainly be avoided, come what may, except perhaps within a strictly medical context. If a person is described as being kept alive by means of a 'life support machine', one realises that he is prevented from dying by being coupled up to a piece of apparatus which has taken over from his own lungs, kidneys or whatever other part of him that is refusing to do its job. But, for an organization to say that 'we provide a life support service to some 10,000 people from 30 different ethnic backgrounds' (*The Daily Telegraph*, 17 Dec 1981) is vague and quite possibly misleading in the extreme. It could mean anything from selling people life assurance to discouraging them from suicide, from food and heating to kidney machines. But it sounds so dignified, so selfless, caring and public spirited, that the experienced observer realises immediately that someone is about to make money in large amounts.

Limited
Small. The word has become an insidious nuisance and an all-too-popular piece of dishonesty. It is often a most regrettable barrier set up between the reader and the truth. What, for instance, is one to make of 'A limited number of Russian transport planes landed in Warsaw during the night curfew' (*New Standard*, 16 Dec 1981)? How many constitutes 'a limited number'? Six? Sixty? One can hardly imagine even the Russians landing 'an unlimited number' of planes. Yet, for some reason, the newspaper cannot bring itself to use such phrases as 'a few' or 'a small number'. This would sound very unimpressive, not worth mentioning, in fact. On the other hand, no newsman likes to appear ignorant. 'Limited' is an ideal word for this kind of occasions, since few people will want to ask 'Exactly how many?' It is a great word for nipping discussion in the bud. A favourite trick among people with goods or services to sell is to encourage the idea of desirable items being in short supply, whether this is true or not. This is unnecessary when tickets are involved, since it must be obvious to anyone that attendance at the Cup Final or at Covent

Garden has to be 'limited', and that only a certain number of people can be got into an aeroplane. There are some branches of commerce, however, in which the situation is more elastic, and where the tactics of 'Hurry, hurry, everybody wants this and delay is dangerous' are considered to be good for business. A package tour company, for instance, may attempt to get bookings by saying 'Space is limited, so don't wait' (*New York Times*, 27 Sept 1981), without giving any indication of whether they have 100 rooms on offer or 10,000, and a company selling Irish sweaters will announce that these goods are 'imported in limited quantities' (*New Yorker*, 31 May 1982). Similarly, Joy de Jean Patou, 'the costliest perfume in the world', is made out to be so rare and so precious that the warning has to go out, 'Limited quantities available' (*New Yorker*, 2 Nov 1981), although who is to know whether this implies that there is only a gallon or a tankerload of the stuff each year for the whole of the USA?

An exceptionally fine illustration of the snob use of 'limited' was provided by the promotors of Smirnoff Czar vodka. This nectar, it explained, was on the market 'in quantities limited by its very nature' (*New Yorker*, 19 Oct 1981). The exact meaning of this masterpiece is worth exploring. Are one's thoughts being directed towards the nature of vodka in general or of Smirnoff Czar vodka in particular? If it is the former, there is possibly a suggestion that, because vodka is so potent — its 'nature' is potency — that it ought, in the national interest, to be kept secret. If the 'nature' is specifically that of Smirnoff Czar vodka, then it is presumably its superior quality which is referred to. Or perhaps its superior price, which might indeed make its appeal 'limited'. But supply, in the case of this particular commodity, is entirely a matter of demand. It can be as high or as low as one pleases. The point at which this is 'limited' is entirely arbitrary.

Living
Exciting, stimulating. These definitions, however, are no more than guesses at the meaning of one of the more idiotic of today's reviewers' words. A typical example of its use is 'A living book, which will surely last a long time in print' (*New Yorker*, 12 July 1982). The book in question is John Julius Norwich's *A History of Venice*, which is a pleasant enough treatment of the subject, but hardly in the song and dance class, if that is how some people might interpret the word. A book which is not 'living' is presumably 'dead', but for some reason this is not found as often as it should be. Yet there is probably some difference in the reviewer's mind between 'living' and 'lively', another opposite of

'dead'. The Bible, if published for the first time today, would undoubtedly be described as a 'living' book, not as 'lively', which would be felt to lack seriousness and depth.

Location
Factory. This is yet another of today's euphemisms for 'factory', a word which has become too obscene to be used in polite society. It occurs in such contexts as 'He or she will also co-ordinate five production locations' (*New York Times*, 27 Sept 1981). A 'production location' is, of course, a factory, and to co-ordinate the work of five factories makes perfect sense. One cannot, however, co-ordinate five 'locations', although what is at or on these locations can certainly be dealt with in this way. *See also* ENVIRONMENT and FACILITY.

Lordship
Ownership. This feudal term has about as much relevance and meaning today as 'thane' or 'folkmoot', but in the phrase 'lordship of the manor', it is adored by house agents, who recognise it as a true friend. So we have, ad nauseam, such encouraging descriptions as 'A fine compact residential and agricultural estate, with 3 Lordships of the Manor' (*Country Life*, 23 June 1982). The sad truth is that '3 Lordships of the Manor' is sheer meaningless nonsense. There are no manors nowadays and consequently no lordships, for the very good reason that England is no longer a feudal society. But it sounds absolutely splendid to say, as estate agents frequently do, that 'the Lordship of the Manor goes with the house'. Every snob in the market is attracted to the place, as flies are to jam.

Luminously
In an illuminating manner, clearly. This began life as an American academic dribble, was gratefully picked up by jargon-thirsty reviewers on that side of the Atlantic and is now showing ominous sights of settling down here. It can always be replaced by a simpler and more straightforward word. In 'The nature and limits of psychological knowledge are so luminously characterised by this quotation' (*American Psychologist*, March 1981), for instance, 'luminously characterised' means, if indeed it means anything, 'clearly indicated', but that would not impress readers of *American Psychologist* to anything like the same extent, conditioned as they are to judging the merit of a thought by the number of syllables taken to describe it.

Luxurious
Better than average. The difficulty with this word is that what was considered luxurious yesterday is normal and expected today, a fact which
can present house agents with problems. An ingenious attempt to get
round the problem has been made in recent years by having both 'luxury'
and 'luxurious' available. 'Luxury' is the ordinary kind, the norm,
'luxurious' is rather better. So all bathrooms are automatically 'luxury
bathrooms' and all flats 'luxury flats', just as, in a different field, all
coaches are 'luxury coaches'. But for a 'luxurious bathroom' — '2 beds,
luxurious bathroom' (*Western Gazette*, 4 June 1982), one would be
expected to pay a good deal more. The bath would be longer, wider and
coloured, the taps would be imitation gold, every tenth tile instead of
every twentieth would have a picture of a ship or a flying duck, and so on.
Every right-minded person recognises the luxurious when he sees it. In
ten years' time, however, the overall standard will have risen, and what
was once 'luxurious' will have become merely 'luxury'. By then, status
will be demanding power-driven towels, hydraulic soap-squirts, lavatory pans which sink into the floor at the touch of a remote control
button and, of course, built-in television. Nothing less will allow the
place to qualify for the accolade of 'luxurious bathroom'.

Luxury
Ordinarily decent. *See* LUXURIOUS. Anything which is not 'luxury' is
now virtually unsaleable, a candidate for a museum. It should be noted,
however, that 'luxury' is never applied, in the house-selling world, to
anything the removals men can take away. 'Luxury' has to be built in, a
more or less permanent fixture. One can therefore speak of a 'luxury
bathroom' or of a 'luxury kitchen' — 'Superbly fitted luxury kitchen'
(*Western Gazette*, 4 June 1982) — but not of a 'luxury bedroom' or
'luxury sitting room', since these are the areas in which the occupier
provides his own luxury or, even better, his own luxuriousness.

M

Major

Leading, big, important. 'Major' had a dishonourable mention in *The Dictionary of Diseased English*, but the situation has deteriorated fast since then and the word now qualifies for a fuller entry here. What is this ever-growing army of 'major' users trying to say? Why do they love the word so much? Consider, for example, 'We are a major manufacturer of industrial chemicals' (*The Daily Telegraph*, 18 Dec 1981). What is this firm trying to say about itself? That it is big, important, occupying a position close to the top of the league? A mixture of all three is probably intended, but 'major' offers an easy way of avoiding certain problems. To say one is 'big' or 'large' would be prosaic, and would encourage the curious to ask 'how big?' 'Important' might be true, but equally it might not and, in any case, the inconvenient question 'How important?' might rear its head. 'Major' fills the bill very nicely. It feels impressive, it carries authority and, above all, it does not open up a discussion. It allows the situation to be kept under control. One can easily and naturally enquire, 'How big?' or 'How important?' but hardly, unless one is exceptionally determined or cynical, 'How major?'

So, 'Our client is a major U.K. independent hospital group' (*The Sunday Times*, 25 Oct 1981), where the unuttered and, with luck, unformed questions are, first, 'How many such groups are there?' and, second, 'How do you rank among them?' Sometimes a little confusion can arise and this offers hope that 'major' may be losing its grip and that, just conceivably, it could be on the way out. 'Our client, a major public company, are (*sic*) leaders (*sic*) in the supply of automotive parts' (*The Daily Telegraph*, 18 Dec 1981) reflects the interesting view that it is possible to be major by being more than one leader at a time, which is reasonable enough, although it is a pity that one has to wreak such grammatical havoc in order to make the point.

Manageable

Not too big. Few people want either an unmanageable house, an unmanageable horse, or unmanageable children, so that 'manageable' is obviously a recommendation. But the term is not an absolute. One is entitled to ask 'manageable by whom?' or 'unmanageable by whom?'

House agents do not, apparently, acknowledge this. They are apt to talk about 'a superbly maintained, individual property of manageable proportions' (*Country Life*, 21 May 1981) and to leave the matter there, as if the right kind of customers would understand immediately what was meant. One may feel entitled to challenge such an assumption. If the property is indeed 'superbly maintained', how many people were required to keep it in this enviable condition? Having prised out this piece of information, one would be in a position to know the number required to make the house and grounds 'manageable'. As it stands, however, the expression amounts to a confidence trick. 'Manageable' by one person? Two? Six? Nothing is just 'manageable'. Even if one replaces this unsatisfactory word by 'not too big', precisely the same objection applies. How big, one wants to know. How many acres, how many bedrooms, how many windows to clean?

Man-management

The management of men. Or so one would have thought, before coming across an advertisement for a production manager, whose task it would be 'to head up a primarily female labour force' for which 'proven man-management ability' was required (*The Daily Telegraph*, 17 Sept 1981). One is reminded of Lord Reith, who, when Director-General of the BBC, once asked his women producers to regard themselves when at work as honorary men. 'Woman-management ability' would, of course, have introduced other than professional considerations and would, for this reason, have been considered an unsuitable phrase, so 'man-management' it has to be, whatever the feminists may say and however ludicrous it may seem for a manager to learn the art of getting the best out of women workers by using men as practice material.

The whole problem could have been avoided if candidates for the post had been asked to provide 'evidence of skill in handling people'. This, however, would have been a layman's way of putting it. For one professional talking to another, it had to be 'man-management', with its bracing military overtones and its suggestion of discipline and firmness, even if the people to whom one happened to have to apply man-management principles were women.

Motivated

Willing to work hard, with an incentive to work. *The Dictionary of*

Diseased English has only a brief note on this word and, since its use has become much more widespread since then, a more detailed examination seems called for now. As always with the jargon of modern management, one must allow for the possibility that, in any given context, 'motivated' may have no meaning whatever and that it has been included for purely liturgical reasons. This would certainly appear to be the case when one is told, in connection with a sales managership for gas turbines, 'this challenging position calls for a highly motivated person' (*The Daily Telegraph*, 6 Jan 1982). The person appointed to fill this vacancy would know perfectly well what his job was. He would be responsible for selling gas turbines in a very competitive market and his employers would be most unlikely to choose anyone who struck them as being idle and lacking in a will to succeed. What, then, is the point of specifying that he must be 'highly motivated'? Everyone concerned could surely take this for granted. The phrase carries no hidden meaning, unless, perhaps, it is a euphemism for 'ambitious' or 'greedy', neither of which could be expressed in such plain terms. The situation is probably similar to that with which prospective headmasters of Victorian public schools were confronted at their interview. They were always asked if they were communicant members of the Church of England, knowing perfectly well that they had no chance whatever of success if they said 'No'. The school governors would not appoint a person who was not a practising Christian, the industrial firm would refuse to consider anyone who confessed to being anything but highly motivated. In both cases, however, there has been an obligation to go through the approved form of words. In the late 1970s, only the Americans were able actually to say in conversation that a person was 'motivated'. The British put it on paper, but only very rarely brought themselves to the point of uttering it. Nowadays, however, the psychological climate is different and apparently normal people can be overheard saying that such and such a person is either 'motivated' or 'lacking in motivation'.

But, spoken or written, 'motivated' is a word society could very well do without. The 'keen young men' of pre-World War II days have been replaced by the 'motivated young man' of today, and it is difficult to attempt to translate into pre-war language such fine-sounding modern pomposities as 'We are seeking a highly-qualified experienced and motivated service educationist' (*The Guardian*, 2 Feb 1982). 'Motivated' might come out as 'genuinely interested in his job', which one could never say, of course, because it would suggest that a high proportion of teachers are played-out timeservers, which indeed they

are. A 'service educationist', for the benefit of those who are not familiar
with the term, is a practising teacher.

Motivation

Willingness to work hard, ambition. *See* MOTIVATED. The reasons for
the motivation are unimportant, the important thing is to have it,
whatever it may be. People work as they do from fear, greed, love of
power and many other emotional forces. The management world does
not see the situation in quite this way. The only kind of 'motivation'
which is fully reputable is a burning, God-given determination to
increase the company's profits. The need to meet one's mortgage
payments would be considered a very minor and even unworthy form of
motivation, and certainly not something which is implied — if anything is
implied — in such sentences from the businessman's phrasebook as
'Drive and motivation are essential qualities for this key appointment'
(*The Daily Telegraph*, 7 Jan 1982), 'motivation' presumably being the
fuel for the drive.

Mouthwatering

Causing the saliva to flow, enticing, attractive, exciting. In the old days,
when words still had meaning, food could be 'mouthwatering' and so, at
a pinch, could a menu or a recipe, which are, so to speak, food at one
remove. Nowadays, however, this ill-treated word is used in a much
wider sense in connection with anything which has the power to excite
the emotions and to suggest future delights. A woman, for instance, can
be 'mouthwatering', with no cannibalistic thoughts in mind, and so can
the contents of a holiday brochure. But 'mouthwatering' has indeed
strayed very far from its original meaning when it is possible to speak of
'a mouthwatering 104 piece set of tableware, cutlery and glassware'
(*Sunday Telegraph*, 13 June 1982). To become excited by staring at
knives and forks must, one would have thought, be somewhat out of the
ordinary, although the association of ideas can, as we know, sometimes
produce extraordinary results.

Multi-instrumental

More than one instrument. An absurd and misleading innovation within
the music business. What does the management of an orchestra mean
when it tells trumpeters who may be considering a job with the orchestra
that 'multi-instrumental capacity is considered a valuable asset' (*The
Guardian*, 2 Feb 1982)? To begin with — *see* CAPACITY — there is a real

difference between 'capacity' and 'ability', and what is required in this case is clearly 'ability', not 'capacity'. But how many additional instruments does a trumpet-player need to be able to perform on before he can be considered 'multi-instrumental'? Would one more be sufficient or does it have to be six, every instrument in the orchestra, or what? One can easily imagine a perfectly good musician wondering if, with only the trumpet, trombone and French horn to offer, his application would receive even a passing glance.

N

Natural

Born to something, ideally suited by nature. Until the mid-1920s a 'natural' was a person naturally deficient in intellect, a half-wit. Then the new meaning of 'someone naturally fitted for a particular role' appeared in the USA, but it was, for some reason, not commonly used in the UK until about 1955. The first meaning has largely dropped out of colloquial use, with the new attitude to what are now called the 'mentally handicapped', but it is still hovering in the wings, as a consequence of its frequent presence in literature. Both Dickens and Hardy, for example, used it without the slightest self-consciousness or feeling of guilt. The second and more recent meaning must by now be part of the normal vocabulary of nearly everyone in the UK, but since about 1980 it has acquired a rather special sense in the commercial and industrial worlds. This is illustrated by 'We want men in their twenties who have proven selling history and who are naturals' (*The Daily Telegraph*, 10 Dec 1981).

It is doubtful if anyone is a 'natural' as a salesman in quite the same way as he might be at flying, teaching or playing a musical instrument. It depends to some extent on what one is required to sell. A good technical representative for computers or machine tools might very well be useless at selling petfoods or the *Encyclopaedia Britannica*. The probability is that, in this particular context, 'naturals' is introduced merely in order to ring the changes on the other cliché, 'professionals', with the extra advantage, so one supposes, of bringing a matey, 'democratic' tone into the sentence. 'This', these 'men in their twenties' with a 'proven selling history' are assured, 'is no starched shirt company. We are all jovial, extrovert naturals here.' But the wily observer is not fooled and, remembering the other meaning of the word, he can give himself the pleasure of a quiet smile at the thought of a firm calling its salesmen half-wits without either of the parties being aware of it.

Natural food

Reared or produced under the conditions supposedly intended by

nature. *See also* HEALTH FOOD, REAL FOOD and WHOLE. The fundamental question one has to ask is, 'How far back does one have to go in
history for the first 'unnatural' foods to appear?' The truth is that all
farming, from Stone Age times onwards, is and always has been to some
extent 'unnatural'. The whole point of farming is that it imposes a
discipline on nature and compels her to do things which, left to her own
devices, she would not do. She would not, for example, plough ground,
confine stock in fenced fields or in buildings, or castrate animals, all of
which are practices which have been going on for a very long time. There
is little that is 'natural' about farming.

What most people mean when they use the word 'natural' in connection with food today is something rather specialized, 'food as it was
produced 100 years ago, before the days of artificial fertilizers, chemical
sprays and battery hens'. This is certainly what is implied by 'Natural
Fresh Eggs' (in large letters on the back of a lorry seen on A303,
England, 23 Aug 1982).

'Health Care, Herbal Remedies, Natural Foods' (advertisement of
shop in Temple Street, Bristol, seen 15 July 1982) defines 'natural'
differently. For this shop, as for many others, 'natural foods' are
essentially vegetarian and essentially uncooked. A 'natural' diet, in this
sense, is one which excludes all forms of meat, fish, eggs and dairy
products, no matter how they are produced. It does, however,
encourage the consumption of profoundly 'unnatural' foods, such as the
cultivated forms of bananas, raisins and nuts, to say nothing of such
highly sophisticated commodities as peanut butter, which one could
search for in vain in nature. 'Natural' is a translator's hell and no easy
ride for the British either.

Neatness
Individual, but discreet flavour. *The Dictionary of Diseased English*
defined the wine-word 'neat' as 'noticeable, but not too prominent'. It
made no mention of 'neatness', which seems to have appeared more
recently and which is equally poetic, infuriating or absurd, according to
one's mood. If wine writers themselves are unable to agree on its
meaning, one seems entitled to ask what chance there is for a mere
outsider? What, for instance, is he to make of such a sentence as 'The
light soil gives a zip and neatness to the whites in particular' (*The Times*,
31 Oct 1981)? These fortunate white wines are, one imagines, with only
the metaphor as a guide, refreshing, not particularly strong and to be
sipped, rather than quaffed.

O

Older style

Not later than 1930, and probably before 1914. There is much to be said for making it compulsory for estate agents to state clearly in all their advertising matter the year in which a house was built. This would free prospective buyers from the need to enter a guessing game and, in not a few instances might make properties easier to sell. A house built between 1900 and 1914, for example, is usually better designed and more solidly constructed than one which was new in the 1920s. Yet both are commonly included under the vague heading, 'older style'.

No-one is able to give a precise or even a reliable answer as to when the 'older style' began and when it ended. Like the Middle Ages and the Renaissance, it just happened. It can, however, make a considerable difference if a house is Early Older Style, Middle Older Style or Late Older Style. Two examples from a single issue of a provincial weekly newspaper illustrate the problem. 'Individual Detached 4-bed 2 reception House in the older style' (*Western Gazette*, 3 March 1982) almost certainly refers to a house built before World War I — it may even be late 19th century — while the 'older style individual 3-bed bungalow' (*Western Gazette*, 3 March 1982) has all the signs of belonging to the 1920s or 1930s. Both have been there for more than half a century and could therefore be fairly called old houses. This, however, is a term no self-respecting estate agent would ever use.

Ongoing

Continuing. This German-American barbarism received fairly full treatment in *The Dictionary of Diseased English*. Since then, there are welcome signs that it is being gradually laughed out of court, at least in the UK. The process is slow, however, and the word retains the affections of two of the worst centres of linguistic corruption, psychology and business management, both of which will no doubt persist with 'ongoing' long after everyone else has abandoned it. An offering of recent vintage from each of these seems appropriate. From the psychologists comes

'The interaction between terminal location and distance cues was uninfluenced by the ongoing activity in the filled retention interval' (*British Journal of Psychology* (1981), 72) and from scientific management, 'The ability to interface effectively with sales and production management at early stages ensuring appropriate ongoing purchasing activity is important' (*The Daily Telegraph*, 5 Nov 1981). In such company as this, 'ongoing' is hardly noticed.

Option
Choice. When *The Dictionary of Diseased English* appeared in 1977, the chief impresarios of 'options' were the car manufacturers, among whom what had formerly been 'extras' were now, more tactfully, 'options'. Since then the word has passed into more general use as a commercial and rather classier synonym for 'choice'. An American catalogue, for instance, exists 'to give you a world of options for home decorating' (*New York Times*, 27 Sept 1981). One should not allow oneself to be bewitched by this modern-sounding word. An 'option' is a choice and nothing more.

Oriental
From the East. Restaurant-keepers have recently begun using this word in contexts where it appears to add little, if anything, to the meaning. A typical example is 'Scampi Provençale, served with Oriental Rice' (menu, Great Northern Hotel, London, July 1982). The New Catering lays down that no noun shall be used without an adjective. The scampi cannot therefore appear on the menu simply as 'served with rice'. This, it is believed, would be far too dull. So 'oriental' is slipped in before the rice. One might feel that, once started on the adjectival track, the restaurant's creative genius could have produced something more exotic and exciting than this. Why not 'Sri Lankan rice' or 'South Korean rice'? It could well be, however, that the Great Northern Hotel had not the faintest idea where the rice came from and that 'oriental' was used because it seemed vague and safe. It makes, of course, absolutely no difference to the taste or appearance of the dish.

Orientated, oriented
Particularly suitable for, directed towards, with an emphasis on. Noted in *The Dictionary of Diseased English* as a marvellous word for mentally lazy people, the appeal of 'orientated' grows steadily year by year. One wonders indeed how the English-speaking world ever managed without it, until the psychologists obligingly discovered it in the 1950s. Until the

late 1970s, 'oriented' was the more popular form, but nowadays the fashion seems to favour 'orientated', at least in the UK. A few examples will show the extent to which the word inhibits clear thinking. One firm in search of management recruits says that 'applicants should be profit-orientated and self-motivated' (*The Birmingham Post*, 5 Nov 1981), which seems an absolutely pointless waste of words, since anyone employed at this level must realize that his job depends on the company making a profit and must be prepared to work hard and sensibly without being perpetually told to do so. The two hyphenated words are there simply because they look and sound impressive and because they have a pleasing rhythm.

One might also reasonably expect a works manager to be good at handling his staff, but it has to be spelt out — 'If you are active, conscientious, even-tempered, adaptable and genuinely people-orientated ...' (*The Daily Telegraph*, 10 Dec 1981). The same paragon, it should be noted, was also required to be 'growth-orientated'. So omni-purpose is this useful word that things, as well as people, can be 'orientated'. One can have, for example, 'a growth-oriented environment where you contributions will be noted and rewarded' (*New York Times*, 27 Sept 1981) and 'a stud and arable farm, orientated towards an equestrian/eventing centre' (*Country Life*, 21 May 1981).

There are times, however, when one longs for the days before 'orientated/oriented' made plain English unnecessary, before 'If you use a computer as a teaching-tool' was replaced by 'If you're a computer-oriented educator' (*New York Times*, 27 Sept 1981).

Orientation
Concern with, interest in, training or experience in. Even more than 'orientated/oriented', the noun attracts pompous people to it like flies to a light. Underneath all the puff and padding, 'The bank has continued to emphasise its customer orientation' (*Financial Times*, 26 Oct 1981) is 'The bank, as always, continues to put its customers' interests first', which may not be true, but does at least provide a firm basis for disagreement. And one can deduce, after a few minutes' reflection, that the university which 'invites applications from persons with student development orientation' (*New York Times*, 27 Sept 1981) is looking for someone who has specialized in helping students to grow intellectually and to get the maximum benefit from their course.

Originally designed
Either just 'designed' or with a quirky or weird and wonderful design. It

is important to know which meaning is intended, in, for instance, 'The outstanding, originally designed, Vacoa Village' (Wings brochure, *Faraway Holidays*, Summer 1983). In the photograph, Vacoa Village, in the Seychelles, looks not unpleasant, although what these holidays habitations are like inside is another matter. But the use of 'originally designed' calls into question what has been happening to the word 'designed'. A postage stamp, for instance, is 'designed', and the 125 high-speed trains are 'designed', in the sense that an artist or a designer sits down and produces his concept of what these objects are to look like. The result may be good or bad, it may be strikingly original or not, but what has been produced will at least be different from anything that has been seen before. However, in an age when so much that is sold is little more than a copy of many other examples of the same kind, with one or two small details changed, to say that something is 'original' is of great importance. This is, perhaps, especially true of clothes, where the 'original', from one of the leading fashion houses, is appallingly expensive, but the mass-produced replicas are within the reach of almost everybody. But, because there are so few genuinely new designs about, one is bound to regard the 'originally designed' Vacoa Village with some suspicion. It all depends on who the 'designer' was, if he existed, and how good he was.

Out of all proportion
Bigger than one might have thought. One can find oneself in a state of fear which is out of all proportion to the real situation and a house can be out of all proportion to the family which lives in it, but it is a little difficult to imagine a motorcar in which the passenger accommodation is out of all proportion to the size of the vehicle. Yet this can apparently be so, as one sees from 'The interior space and comfort for five is out of all proportion to the Cavalier's overall size' (promotion leaflet for the Vauxhall Cavalier car, issued by Gordale Co., Bingley, Yorkshire, England, Dec 1982). If the Cavalier were able to transport a full-sized elephant with ease, the interior space would indeed be out of proportion to the overall size. All that is really meant, however, is that the car can take five people in above-average comfort.

P

Passenger product

Seat on an aeroplane, train, coach; cabin on a ship. One could be excused for not thinking this a particularly graceful term, but it exists and it certainly deserves careful examination. In any form of business, what one is trying to sell is nowadays known as 'the product'. It may be bibles or tins of sardines, pork pies or foreign stamps, To the businessman, all goods are potentially equal. Their value is determined by their profitability, not by their social or cultural importance.

A transport undertaking can prosper only by the successful marketing of its freight or passenger services, which constitute its 'product'. It does, even so, come as something of a shock to observe that additional representatives are required 'to sell the KLM worldwide passenger product' (*The Daily Telegraph*, 19 Feb 1982), not least because, to the uninitiated, 'passenger product' may well suggest what passengers produce, and to sell that would indeed by a specialized and skilled task.

Pathbreaking

Pioneering. Or at least one supposes this is what is meant. The word is a literal translation from the German, *'bahnbrechend'* and sits awkwardly in English. What, one wonders, is suddenly wrong with 'pioneering' after all these years? The answer is to be found by looking at the kind of people who are most fond of the word, literary critics and reviewers and religious enthusiasts of the more fervid and evangelistic kind. This clumsy-sounding word seems to have originated in the USA in the 1960s, but it is now showing signs of spreading elsewhere. It nearly always has sentimental, walking-towards-the-dawn overtones, as in 'This truly pathbreaking book' (*New York Review of Books*, 3 Dec 1981), where there would also appear to be just a little exaggeration.

Peer-review

A review by one's professional equals. Many, perhaps most authors would feel that the people who review their books are, by temperament,

95

intellect or interests, ill-qualified to do so. Sometimes, alas, this is true. But novelists, biographers and other people who write with the general public in mind would be extremely unlikely to say that they yearn for 'peer-reviewers'. This curious, not to say pedantic term is a virtual monopoly of the academics, whose career is able to progress only if sufficient of their 'peers' agree that their work is fit to publish. Even after publication, other 'peers' may well decide that it is full of mistakes and that the world of scholarship would have been a sweeter and better place if it had never been published at all. One's 'peers' can be not unlike members of the Holy Inquisition, appointed by God to root out heresy and error and many a gentle soul has been led to the brink of suicide by a really savage 'peer-review'. However, such things are evidently reckoned to be a good and bracing element in academic life and scholarly periodicals take great pride in promising their readers 'rigorous peer-reviews by an editorial board of national and international experts' (mailing by Baywood Publishing Co., Farmingdale, New York, 1981).

People-orientated
Interested in people. *See* ORIENTATED. Until recently, employers used to require of candidates for certain secretarial jobs that they should be 'interested in people'. How they have to be 'people-orientated', to show that the firm has moved with the times. But both expressions mean exactly the same, that visitors drift in and out of the premises all the time and that, with luck, one might occasionally have a chance to speak to one or two of them. The secretary who is totally 'people-orientated', that is, interested in nothing but people, could, however, prove a little difficult to have around the place.

Per cent
Considerable. The passion for quantifying is one of the diseases of the age and the advertisers are only too willing to encourage it, knowing full well that nothing sells as well as what looks like science. We therefore find car makers indulging in such plausible nonsense as 'Latest results show a 48% average improvement in quality over 1980 models as reported by new car owners' (*New Yorker*, 17 May 1982). That happened to be Ford but, in this as in other matters, others follow where Ford leads, and by no means only in car manufacturing. To prevent oneself from falling into the hypnotic state induced by such an advertisement, it is helpful to look carefully and objectively at this '48% average improvement in quality over 1980 models'. What does it mean? What

can it mean? An improvement in petrol consumption can be measured, but an improvement in quality cannot, unless 'improvement in quality' is another and more flattering way of saying 'decrease in the number of complaints, breakdowns, component failures or times the guarantee is invoked'. This probably comes somewhere near the truth of the situation, but for a car manufacturer to say publicly that its 1981 models had only half the number of breakdowns per 10,000 miles by comparison with the cars produced the previous year would do the public image of Ford or whomsoever absolutely no good at all. Much safer to turn the whole situation round and blind the reader with science, even if it happens to be bogus science.

Perception
Considered opinion. Social scientists and their friends and allies are very fond of 'perception', and it is not difficult to see why. To speak or write of someone's 'perception', even if one means no more than his opinion, is to suggest insight, the ability to see below the surface of things and to sense relationships which are hidden from lesser men. 'Perception', in short, is a flattering word, and 'opinion' is not.

One therefore finds a supposedly learned journal referring to 'the perception of many legislators' (*American Journal of Psychiatry*, 138, 12 Dec 1981). This does not imply, as one might think, that the nation's congressmen or even senators are men of distinguished intellect and remarkable intuition. All the writer is trying to say — and professional etiquette prevents him from expressing himself in simple terms — is 'this is the way many of our politicians see the situation', and that way, of course, is not necessarily perceptive at all. Other examples, however, make much heavier demands on one's abilities as a translator. A really advanced test piece would be 'Only original papers are published dealing with supported perceptions of educational technology systems' (mailing by Baywood Publishing Company, Farmingdale, New York, 1981). A 'supported perception' has all the appearance of coming from the world of architecture or civil engineering, but one could probably replace it by 'well-documented opinion' without doing anybody a serious injustice. But a man with 'supposed perceptions' is clearly destined to reach the academic heights, whereas one with no more than 'well-documented opinions' will never rise above the level of a reliable plodder.

Perceptive
Knowing the cause, able to dig below the surface. As *The Dictionary of*

Diseased English observed, this has become part of the novel-reviewer's stock-in-trade and one can hardly go wrong with it, since no-one is likely to be offended by being called 'perceptive' and, since the word has no precise meaning, the reviewer cannot be attacked for incompetence. It is possible to feel, even so, that 'perceptive' is frequently used merely because every noun deserves an adjective, and that it contributes remarkably little to one's understanding of the book or of what is going on in the reviewer's mind. In 'He treats feminist attacks on romance with perceptive sympathy' (*New York Review of Books*, 3 Dec 1981), for instance, one wonders just what difference there may be between 'perceptive sympathy' and the ordinary kind. Is anything more than simple 'sympathy' required or expected? Or, does the word possibly have the sense of 'indulgent' here? Is there perhaps a patronising attitude hovering around the sentence? It is impossible to be sure with such a silly word.

Period

Between about 1400 and 1850. One can never be quite sure when 'period', a word generously applied to houses, furniture and clothes, begins and ends. The 1920s are a little too recent for it, although it is difficult to say quite why, and one never refers to a Roman toga or a Saxon kilt as 'period dress'. 'Period furniture' is Tudor to very early Victorian and a 'period house' is roughly the same. But there can be problems, as with 'an attractive period village house' (*Country Life*, 21 May 1981). Is it 'a village house built in an attractive period', 'an attractive house in a period village', or 'an attractive period house in a village'? Or is everything attractive? One can hardly decide on paper. A journey is clearly necessary in order to clear matters up.

A personal check is also advisable if one should happen to be considering buying 'a magnificent Period refurbished flat' in Gloucester Square, London (advertisement by Chestertons, *London Portrait*, Jan 1983). Is the flat in a period house, and, if so, of what period is it? Or is one being offered a period refurbishment? One could quite easily have a 20th-century flat in an 18th-century house, or vice versa. Sometimes house agents appear to have lost faith in the pulling power of 'period' and throw it in as a make-weight, with the real selling job to be done by other key words in the sentence. This is well illustrated by 'A magnificent 18th century Grade II listed period house' (*London Portrait*, Jan 1983), which pulls out all the stops on the organ.

Perspective
Advantages? Length? Breadth? Used in the way social scientists use it, this word has reached the point at which it should be suppressed by law. It encourages people with nothing to say to believe that they have an important message to give to the world. Examples abound and this one is no worse than many others — 'The rewards can be meaningful and numerous in terms of total educational perspective, self image and future career goals' (*New York Times*, 27 Sept 1981). This sentence is almost untranslatable. It refers to a course in business management. What, one has a right to know, is the 'total educational perspective' the course offers? Does it mean that the course is not narrow in its concept, that one's 'total education' will benefit from it, that its long-term results will be profound? Or is it there in the prospectus just to look good and to ensnare innocent students and their parents?

Personalised
For you alone. In a world in which everything is mass-produced and in which individual tastes and needs have ceased to matter, there is money to be made by offering something just a little different, even if the personal element in the goods or the transaction turns out to be illusory. The important thing about 'personalisation', one gathers, is not that one is actually being treated as an individual, a one-off, but one shall feel that one is. Consider the bank which says that it 'provides you, the private investor, with an unrivalled range of personalised financial services' (*Swissair Gazette*, Oct 1981). What this bank, like any other, is providing, is 'financial services'. These services include advice on investments, which may involve meeting a member of the bank's staff from time to time. But there is nothing new or special about this. If one is summoned to the bank to explain the unwelcome size of one's overdraft, one is receiving 'personalised service', although nobody ever refers to it in these terms. 'Personalised service' is, in fact, an expression used mainly to flatter the rich, who like to feel that they are not being treated like the rest of their fellow citizens, and those who are not exactly rich but who purr with pleasure at the thought of being considered so.

Personnel
People. In order to present a disciplined, military front to the world, an industrial concern is liable to reveal that it has 'a department of approximately fifty personnel' (*The Daily Telegraph*, 17 Sept 1981), when any normal person would say 'fifty people'. If a department can have fifty 'personnel', then presumably it can have one, and, this being so,

'personnel' is both singular and plural, which is an interesting development. To the managerial mind, however, 'personnel' are not exactly people. They are people-on-the-payroll, a special human breed, normally thought of as a collective. One could hardly attend an ordinary dinner party for fifty personnel, but it might just be possible to say that there were 'fifty personnel in the works canteen' and get away with it.

Pianism

Feeling for the piano, style. This rather affected term is fortunately confined to music critics, who are capable of such sentences as 'His most aristocratic pianism came in a group of Debussy ...' (*The Times*, 5 Jan 1982). The use of 'pianism' assumes a sympathetic reader. It is a code-word to be exchanged between equals, not a method of communicating with the general public. In most cases, 'playing', 'style' or 'technique' would allow the point to be made with more certainty, but without the strong hint of connoisseurship and musical freemasonry which 'pianism' suggests.

It is, by the way, interesting to note that no corresponding word so far exists for other instruments. Knowledgeable people do not refer to 'trombonism', 'oboeism' or 'violinism'. Why pianists and the piano should be so greatly favoured is not clear.

Platter

A dish. Restaurants with pretensions to be a good deal better than they really are have become very fond of serving food on what the menu calls 'platters'. The reason is not far to seek. 'Platter', with its Tudor and medieval associations, suggests good, plain food in large quantities. It is an excellent brainwashing word, invaluable for restaurants which serve very ordinary food and make heavy use of the printed menu to grade it up. So one finds 'a platter of cheese' (menu, Park Lane Hotel, London, July 1982), and 'Fried seafood platter' (menu, Berni Oliver, Bath, England, July 1982). In the old days it would have been just 'cheese' and 'fried fish'. 'Platter makes all the difference. It stimulates the appetite and adds a touch of class to the meal.

Position

Person in a position. Despite its growing popularity, the temptation to misuse 'position' in this way needs to be resisted. A person is not a position and to identify a man completely with his job, so that he has no meaning or existence without it, is a dangerous development. 'Both positions,' announces one firm, 'will perform a full spectrum of sales activities within a regional sales function' (*The Daily Telegraph*, 18 Feb 1982), which is not unlike saying that the Post Office arrives at one's door with the letters.

Positive

Real, saying yes, definite. Remarking that 'positive' in many instances meant absolutely nothing at all, *The Dictionary of Diseased English* went on to say that it was a word 'from which we could do with a long rest'. After six years, one has to report that the situation has in no way improved. 'Positive' is still, in the majority of cases, completely redundant and there is no sign whatever of it being put out to grass. In the hope, however, that this happy retirement will not be long delayed, a few more examples are given here, as an indication of how urgent the pensioning-off process is.

Ambitious electrical engineers are told that, if they should happen to be the right type, 'you'll also have the solid skills and experience necessary to make a positive contribution' (*The Daily Telegraph*, 29 Jan 1982). 'An important contribution' would make sense and so would 'a useful contribution', but 'a positive contribution' seems hardly worth saying, since 'a negative contribution' would amount to sabotage and it should not be necessary to warn prospective employees about this. 'Reaction in Rome', reported the BBC's correspondent, 'was said to be positive' (BBC Radio 4, 8 am News, 11 Nov 1982), which is a journalist's upstage way of saying that the Italian government was in favour of the idea. The same sense of the word can be seen in a sentence from another of the BBC's reporters 'Mr Weinberger thought the Egyptian government's reaction to the plan was a positive sign' (BBC Radio 4, 8 am News, 4 Sept 1982). For 'positive', read 'good' or 'favourable'.

'He has made a major positive effort to advance method and theory' (*Recent Titles in Archaeology*, catalogue issued by Academic Press, New York, 1981) is particularly silly. 'A major effort' is all that can be expected of any academic or archaeologist, and one finds it difficult to imagine this effort being planned so as to lead everyone backwards or to be wholly destructive, which is what 'a negative effort' would mean. What conceivable reason can there be, then, for including 'positive' at all? What point does it make, what extra strength does it give either to 'major' or to 'effort'?

The same kind of question occurs to me after reading, or trying to read, the following piece of pompous tomfoolery. We are told of a successful firm that 'it has built up a high reputation by a positive approach to providing a comprehensive packaging service to a wide range of industries' (*The Daily Telegraph*, 17 Dec 1981). It has done nothing of the sort. Its reputation is the result of 'providing a comprehensive packaging service'. The 'positive approach', whatever that may mean, has nothing to do with the matter. It is sheer makeweight.

But 'The Power of Positive Dieting' (*Boston Globe*, 11 Oct 1981) is the biggest swindle of them all, a final proof of the need to take the word firmly by the hand and show it the door. What this book is all about and what it should be called is 'The Power of Dieting', in other words, the benefits which can result from careful attention to one's diet. There are many different kinds of dietary regime, but 'positive dieting' does not and cannot exist. One can have determined dieting, scientifically planned dieting, drastic dieting, medically supervised dieting, foolish dieting, suicidal dieting and a dozen others, but not positive dieting. It sounds impressive, but it is, alas, as meaningless as 'positive vetting' for potential security risks, and 'positive professionalism' as in 'Shands can offer you the positive professionalism associated with a major teaching hospital' (*New York Times*, 27 Sept 1981).

Positively
Definitely, in the hoped for direction, decisively, strongly, with certainty. To use 'positive' or 'positively' with so many meanings is to impoverish the English language and to move it further towards Basic. It is also to increase the possibility of misunderstanding. What, for example, is really intended when a management recruit is told that he must 'have the ability to positively influence a changing organisation' (*The Sunday Times*, 14 March 1982). Is he to influence the organisation strongly, in a desirable direction, unmistakably? Or is 'positively influence' the new, fashionable way of saying 'influence', just as 'positively identified' may be Modernese for 'identified'? People are always being 'positively identified' nowadays, although quite what 'positively' does to help communication is problematical. 'His father will be coming to London in order that the boy may be positively identified' (BBC Radio 4, 8 am News, 31 Oct 1981) means nothing more or less than the father will identify his son.

Precious
Rare, expensive. The word is much used of materials nowadays. Fabrics, especially silks, are 'precious' and so are certain cabinetmaking woods. A furniture firm may advertise its wares by referring to 'the rich tones of precious Honduras Mahogany' (*New York Times*, 27 Sept 1981). 'Precious Honduras Mahogany' is not 'precious' in quite the same way

as 'precious Chinese silks' is. The silks are precious because its method of production makes silk expensive. The mahogany is 'precious' because there is very little of it available today. Rapacious cutting has reduced supplies to a point at which one might as well have one's furniture made of silver.

Premium

Not the ordinary kind. 'Premium' can mean whatever the manufacturers and advertisers choose it to mean and no-one is likely to be prosecuted for using the word in a deceiving manner, simply because it cannot be defined, except as a technical term employed by stockbrokers and financial journalists and those buying and selling houses. Shares can be 'at a premium', that is, at more than the issue price, and one may be required to pay 'a premium' in order to have one's application to buy living accommodation considered. In these contexts, the meaning of 'premium' is quite clear.

The same cannot be said, however, of 'the finest premium Scotch' (*New Yorker*, 14 June 1982). There is blended Scotch whisky and a noble range of single malts. Some of the whiskies on sale are older than others. Some, undoubtedly, are better than others and for these one can reasonably be expected to pay a higher price. To those who know anything about whisky at all, this makes sense. But 'the finest premium Scotch' does not. Neither, for that matter, does 'the finest Scotch'. If one felt exceptionally kind and generous one might possibly translate 'the finest premium Scotch' as 'blended Scotch whisky of good quality', but that would be about as far as one could go, although this kind of honest truth would probably sell very little whisky.

Presence

Industrial or commercial location. Not long ago, 'presence' was a political and governmental term. One talked, for example, about 'the British presence in India', or 'the American presence in Vietnam'. 'Presence' is also a useful quality for a person in authority to possess. Judges, statesmen and headmasters, for example, carry out their functions a good deal more easily if they have 'presence'. If one brings both these meanings of 'presence' into the same focus, 'presence' emerges not only as 'being in a certain place', but being there impressively and with authority.

In recent years, commerce and industry have been showing distinct signs of megalomania, one of which is the belief that they rule the world, that is, that they are indistinguishable from government and possibly superior to it. As an expression of this, they have taken over words previously identified with the state and the older-established professions. 'Presence' is such a word. This takeover process is to be seen very widely nowadays. One bank, for instance, will speak of its 'growing international presence' (*Financial Times*, 26 Oct 1981) and another will refer to 'the opening of a branch in Osaka, which is an important addition to our well-established presence in Tokyo' (*Financial Times*, 26 Oct 1981). In this last example, 'presence' could perfectly well be replaced by 'business', but 'presence', no doubt, is reckoned to sound grander and more spiritual. 'Presence' is also a euphemism for 'business' in 'This year one of the foremost names of the US $ multi-million domestic electrical appliance market will be developing its existing presence in the U.K. and Europe' (*The Daily Telegraph*, 18 Feb 1982).

For ingenuity and possibly arrogance as well, one should, however, award a 'specially commended' certificate to the perfume manufacturer who claims to sell 'the fragrance with the most exceptional of qualities, presence' (*New Yorker*, 5 July 1982). One gets the point: the fragrance is impressive, it has style, and it is, naturally, expensive. But, to the irreverent, certain other possibilities suggest themselves. The 'presence' could be of an unwelcome kind. One could notice it a long way off and it might require several days to clear a room of all traces of it.

Presentation

Appearance. A house agents' word of very vague meaning indeed. A typical example is the attempt to sell 'a distinguished country house of very high quality and presentation' (*Country Life*, 21 May 1981). What, one wonders, would a prospective buyer understand by 'high quality and presentation'? Does 'quality' refer to the architecture, the workmanship, or the local prestige of the house? If the answer is, at least in part, 'the architecture', then what is left for 'presentation'? Might the 'presentation' of a house conceivably mean its natural environment, the trees, bushes and lawns surrounding it? Or could it be the house agent's presentation, the way he writes it up and promotes it? If this is the answer, it would seem a trifle immodest for the agent to give public praise to his own puff.

It is possible, however, that 'presentation' means nothing more than 'state of decoration' or 'effect of the decorations on the eye'. *See also* PRESENTED.

Presented

Decorated, as it appears with its decorations, carpets, curtains and lighting fitments. The word is applied by house agents only to what they would term 'superior', that is, 'more expensive' properties and, so far, it is little found outside London and one or two of the more fashionable provincial towns. It has no particular value on its own. The adverb which precedes it is everything — 'A beautifully presented house with a south facing garden' (advertisement by McKenzie Ide and Company, *London Property*, mid-Jan 1983); 'Fabulous garden flat impeccably presented for immediate occupation' (advertisement by Faron Sutaria, *London Property*, mid-Jan 1983).

Prestigious

Expensive, bought or used by fashionable people. For something to be 'prestigious', there is nearly always the need for money to change hands, the most important exceptions being names. Harrods, for example, carries a 'prestigious' name and so do the Duke of Norfolk and the Savoy Hotel. What is implied, however, in 'We have a prestigious range of property in and around Marbella' (*Sunday Telegraph*, 24 Jan 1982) is quite different. The property concerned consists of newly built flats and houses. They are 'prestigious' only because the entrepreneurs and their agents have decided that it shall be so. The prestige began on a type-writer and, if the gullible buyer chooses to believe that he is living in 'prestigious' accommodation, and has been willing to pay extra for the word, a fool and his money have been soon and easily parted. There is, of course, a special breed of humanity which spends its life moving from one 'prestigious' thing to another, and there is no shortage of rogues anxious to be of service to them.

Preventive maintenance

Maintenance. This curious term is displayed prominently by British Rail on the sheds where routine maintenance is carried out on waggons and coaches. It was observed outside Temple Meads station, Bristol, England, on 1 Dec 1982. Many thousands of passengers each week must notice it and British Rail, no doubt, hopes that they will find it interesting and reassuring. Some, however, may wonder what exactly it means, since the whole point of ordinary maintenance is to keep a vehicle in good repair and running order and so to forestall trouble. What more could 'preventive maintenance' achieve? One suspects that, like ESSEN-TIAL ENGINEERING, it is part of a British Rail public relations campaign to emphasize that, in these hard times, only work which is absolutely necessary is being carried out. How many passengers react in the way which is expected of them is difficult to say, but one could guess that the number is distressingly small.

Price-sensitive

Likely to influence the price of something. This clumsy phrase is much used in the commercial world nowadays. A typical example would be, 'I'm afraid I can't answer that question. It's price.sensitive' (BBC Radio 4, *The World at One*, 19 March 1982). On this occasion a spokesman for the Midland Bank was trying to explain that anything other than a vague answer from him might affect the value of the Bank's shares. In that case, it was not the question which was price-sensitive, but his reply to it. Had he said, 'The matter's price-sensitive', the situation would have been made clearer, but not as clear as if he had dropped this ridiculous jargon and told his interviewer in plain terms, 'I have to be careful not to say anything which might affect the value of the Bank's shares'. Very few of the listeners to *The World At One* would, one might well think, have had the faintest idea of what 'It's price-sensitive' meant. Perhaps that was the intention.

Prime

Top quality. If its Latin origin means anything at all, 'prime' must mean 'first', and consequently anything which is 'prime' should be the very best that money can buy. It is a rash and often, one fears, untruthful statement, especially where meat is concerned. In the USA it is almost impossible to discover a restaurant where the beef is not 'prime', which makes one wonder where all the rest goes. It has been said in defence of the suppliers of meat that 'prime' does not necessarily mean that the beef or whatever is the best on the market, but that it is 'in prime condition'. Since very tough meat can be 'in prime condition', that is, as good as it is going to get, 'prime' does not, from the customer's point of view, appear to be a very useful word. It may even cause him to think that the meat is better than it actually is, and that could be synonymous with fraud. Fraud, however, is a matter of deliberate intention to deceive and this is often difficult to prove, especially since many restaurants are unable to distinguish between good and inferior meat. Legally, the point at issue is whether, with the words on the menu to guide him, a customer receives what he expects to receive. If he is promised 'a prime rump steak' (Berni Oliver, Bath, England, 6 July 1982), what would he reckon to get? The answer most probably is 'a steak which is not tough' and, if he were given this, he would be very unlikely to complain about either the steak or the word 'prime', which is only there because every menu-noun has to have its adjective, and 'prime' is as good as any.

Prime mover
An initial source of motive power. An electric motor and a steam engine are both prime movers and so, in an emergency, is someone who gives an obstinate car a push downhill to help it to start, but the widespread use of 'prime mover' to describe a person who initiates a business deal is irritating and absurd. If a sales representative is required to possess 'the ability to operate as a prime mover in opening new profitable accounts' (*Sunday Telegraph*, 3 Jan 1982), all that is being asked of him is that he shall get important new customers without needing any help, a normal commercial process, glorified by such powerful-sounding language as 'operate as a prime mover'. But who, one might ask, wants to be thought of as a steam engine or a waterwheel?

Prior
Previous. 'Prior' is, for some extraordinary reason, considered crisper, more businesslike and more professional than 'previous'. It has the additional advantage of being a lawyer's term. When used in the industrial/commercial field, however, it is totally unnecessary in nine cases out of ten, and included purely for effect. 'Prior field engineering/sales experience is desirable' (*The Daily Telegraph*, 18 Feb 1982) means 'field engineering/sales experience is desirable'. All experience is necessarily in the past and therefore 'prior' adds nothing whatever to the message.

Prizewinning
Having won a prize. *See* AWARD-WINNING. Or so one would expect. At one time this expression was used fairly honestly by specifying what prizes had been won and where. Manufacturers of beer, cheese or pork pies would very sensibly advertise the fact that their wares had received awards at an international exhibition in Berlin in 1897 or in Paris in 1903. It was true, provable and good for business.

The modern habit is different. The manufacturers make the claim without supplying the evidence, as in 'Our prizewinning sausages' (menu, Garners Steak House, Leicester Square, London, July 1982). If one asks at the Steak House exactly what prize these sausages have won, the probability is that the manager will be embarrassed. He may, if he is exceptionally quick-witted, reply that 'prizewinning' does not mean that the sausages have actually won a prize but, such is their quality, that they are capable of doing so. One would, however, need to be very simple indeed to fall for that one.

Procurement

Buying. Long ago, in the golden age of commerce, 'buying' and 'selling' were considered honourable terms and no-one felt obliged to search around for euphemistic alternatives. To 'procure', however, had sinister overtones. Unpleasant people existed, whose business was to 'procure' girls to satisfy the lusts of the rich, and a 'procuress' was not a highly regarded figure in society. All this has now changed, and an ambitious person may be told that 'some experience in the procurement of frozen meat and other frozen foods is a definite advantage' (*The Daily Telegraph*, 6 Jan 1982). Assuming, as one should, that the frozen meat is bought, not stolen — 'procurement' covers both possibilities equally well — why does it have to be the pretentious 'procurement', not the honest, straightforward 'buying'? Are we reaching the point where people go out to 'procure' their food, instead of to 'buy' it?

Professional

Someone who takes the job seriously, who has specialized experience and possibly formal qualifications, an expert. Nowadays, this is a very loosely used term and it can easily mislead those who are in the habit of taking words at their face value. The true professions are those which can be practised only by those who have satisfied an examining body that they have followed an approved course of training and reached a satisfactory level of competence. Such people will be registered and their continued membership of the profession will be conditional on observing clearly understood rules of behaviour and skill. In the UK, the 'professions' therefore include doctors, dentists, pharmacists, lawyers and actuaries. They do not include teachers, architects, actors, journalists and engineers, however often one may talk of 'the profession of journalism' or refer to an actor as 'a true professional'. Anyone is free to work as a teacher, journalist or architect.

There are also what one might call the 'near-professions' and the 'would-be professions'. Teaching and museum work are near-professions, insurance and public relations are would-be professions. It is useful to have and to understand these distinctions, although, since the true professions offer, for the most part, security, social prestige and a higher than average income, one can well understand the anxiety of many other kinds of people to get on the professional band-waggon. For this reason, it is always wise to think very hard before deciding what kind of 'professional', if any, one is being offered. Very frequently, one will find that 'professional' can be translated by 'expert', as in the case of 'a professional burglar'. 'A mobile team of banking professionals' (*Financial Times*, 26 Oct 1981) is a group of people with expert banking knowledge and 'a professional in marketing or commercial management' (*The Daily Telegraph*, 12 Jan 1982) is a person who specializes in these fields.

So it is, too, with 'a further professional to join our expanding team which advises clients on distribution and transportation problems' (*The Sunday Times*, 25 Oct 1981). The organization of distribution and transport is not a profession. Anybody is free to engage in it, and this particular team is therefore made up of specialists and experts, not of professionals. 'To invest in Japan like a professional, see Nikko' (*Financial Times*, 26 Oct 1981) is more complicated. There are certainly professional investors, as there are professional boxers and professional gamblers, in the sense of people who make their living in this way and who have, through long experience, acquired great expertise in their chosen calling. What this reference to Nikko means is rather different. Nikko is a Japanese banking and consultancy firm and what they are inviting innocent Westerners to do here is to have their investments in Japan looked after by Nikko, who are experts in such matters, not to become 'professionals' themselves.

It is interesting to notice that 'professional', as a tribute to skill and knowledge, is never applied to members of the professions. One would not say that a doctor or a barrister was 'a true professional', or that he had 'a professional attitude' to his work. The adjective is reserved for those who are outside the professions and one should be suspicious of it for this reason.

Professionalism

Knowing what one is about, being an expert. This is a sadly misused word, calculated to impress those who are ripe for such treatment. The firm which announces that it employs only 'consultants with a worldwide reputation for professionalism' (*The Daily Telegraph*, 11 Dec 1981) is really saying that its staff know their subject backwards and inside-out and apply their knowledge in a careful, methodical way. One could say exactly the same about a first-class motor mechanic or television service engineer. Their 'professionalism' is their expertise.

Profile
Level. 'Profile' is a fashionable word, which is meant to make what one is saying sound more scientific. Often it can be omitted from the sentence altogether, with no change or weakening of meaning. Often, too, the person using 'profile' appears to have only a very vague idea of what it means. 'The high age profile of so many of our drivers' (letter to *The Times*, 16 Aug 1982) from a member of the British Rail Board) means 'The high age of so many of our drivers'. 'Profile' adds nothing to what the writer of the letter is trying to say. He is, in fact, a victim of his anxiety to sound up-to-date and to speak as a modern manager should speak. He has the correct jargon word, but he does not know how to use it. One could properly refer to 'the age profile of our drivers'. The 'profile' in this case would be a diagram showing at a glance what proportion of drivers were between, say, the ages of 30 and 40, 40 and 50 and so on. But 'the high age profile' is meaningless.

Q

Quality
Better than average. Commenting on the interesting fact that 'quality' has come to mean 'good quality', *The Dictionary of Diseased English* noted that 'in the commercial world nothing is ever of bad quality, so that the use of the word 'good' is unnecessary'. This is as true now as it was then, but year by year 'quality' is attached to an increasingly strange variety of nouns. 'Could you sell quality wine part-time?' (*The Daily Telegraph*, 15 June 1982) is fairly straightforward — the wine is presumably not plonk and may even be *appelation contrôlée*. 'To bring quality living into your home' (*New Yorker*, 5 Oct 1981) presents greater problems. It occurred in an advertisement for furnishing fabrics and the thought that the quality of one's life is dependent on one's curtains is an interesting one. A room can certainly be made more pleasant by having some nice new curtains and perhaps fresh covers on the chairs as well, but for this actually to bring 'quality' into lives where there was none before is a cause for wonder. But, since advertisements never lie, there the matter must be allowed to rest.

It is always a useful exercise, when faced with 'quality wine', 'quality living' or quality anything else, to ask oneself what the opposite would be. Would it be *vin ordinaire*, undrinkable wine or what? Dreary living? Mentally and spiritually impoverished living? Living on the fringe of suicide? And so it is with 'quality disposable health-care products' (*The Sunday Times*, 25 Oct 1981). Leaving aside the problems of defining 'health-care products' — this dreadful American expression covers everything from toothpicks to sticking plaster — if they are not 'quality', are they unreliable, inefficient, made of dangerous materials? What does sticking plaster which is not 'quality' do or not do? Fall off immediately? Become permanently welded to the skin?

But the word is already in decline, vague and bloodless, when it is possible to say 'Canvas Holidays continue to be by far the largest quality operator of all-inclusive camp/ferry/hotel holidays in Europe' (*Sunday Telegraph*, 20 Dec 1981). One has adjusted oneself by now to the idea of a 'quality holiday', but the thought of a 'quality operator' brings quite a different set of considerations into play. Such a person would never go back on his promises, never exchange one holiday for another at the last moment, never go bankrupt, never impose surcharges. One is bound to wonder if Canvas Holidays was deliberately trying to turn one's mind in this direction, or whether the whole thing was just a terrible mistake. Such are the pitfalls of 'quality'.

R

Racist

Hostile or prejudicial to coloured people. This is one of the most emotive words of our time, occupying much the same position as 'atheist' did during the Victorian period. Both words constituted a serious barrier to clear thinking and in due course 'racist' will no doubt lose its dangerous force just as 'atheist' did. Meanwhile, however, every possible attempt should be made to avoid using both 'racist' and 'racism', since they do nothing to help to improve the social situation which has given rise to them.

'Racist' is a diseased word. It is based on a passionately held belief that there is no difference whatever between whites and non-whites and that the only behaviour appropriate to a civilized person is to ignore colour altogether and to resist all attempts to draw attention to it. There is a certain amount of sense and fairness in this attitude. Common decency demands that non-whites should not be excluded from shops, restaurants or football matches simply because of their colour. To do so would be to behave in the barbarous fashion of the Nazis towards the Jews. But to pretend that black people, or for that matter brown or yellow people, do not have special problems within British society is to blind oneself to the facts and to withdraw from these people the kind of help and attention to which they are entitled. It is, for example, very necessary that the Department of Employment should possess accurate information about the number of non-whites who are unemployed. Without such information there is no possibility of working out a constructive policy. Yet no sooner had the Employment Secretary issued instructions to his officials that they should collect and register these details than a barrage of angry opposition was laid down, with newspapers reporting that 'The Unions have described the new procedure as "racist" and "wholly obnoxious"' (*Sunday Telegraph*, 23 Jan 1983). What the new procedure is in fact intended to do is to put an end to the previous unsatisfactory situation in which policy had to be based on wholly unscientific evidence. The unions, one suspects, have their own reasons for preferring that the evidence should continue to be unscientific. If the results of a careful, reliable investigation should show, as seems quite likely, that a high proportion of the unemployed were in fact coloured, then the unions would have to change their political strategy, which at present depends on the much more explosive assumption that the typical unemployed person is white. 'Racist' is an extremely convenient word with which to nip a politically awkward investigation in the bud.

There are, however, numerous occasions on which 'racist' has real meaning, although it applies to situations which existed and were dealt with long before the word itself became fashionable. The headline, 'Court told racist taunts led to fight' (*Western Gazette*, 28 Jan 1983) draws the attention of the reader to the story in which the taunts in question were given verbatim. They included, 'Right, you black bastard', a term of abuse which, like 'Right, you yellow bastard', must have been used fairly frequently for a century and more in places where the different races have been forced to mingle. No doubt, 'Right, you white bastard' has been heard now and again, too. One should, however, remember that 'bastard', black or white, is a fearful insult among the British working classes. It is a nice point, worthy of considerable research, as to whether 'black' or 'bastard' was the stronger word on this occasion. It could be that, if two white men had been involved, 'Right, you bastard', would have produced a precisely similar result. But, for the local paper sub, 'racist taunts' were far better copy than mere 'taunts'.

Ranked

Possibly, considered by some. For the word to have any meaning, one needs to know who does the ranking. To say of a Japanese watch that it is 'ranked among the world's great possessions' (*New Yorker*, 20 Dec 1982) may be good advertising but it is linguistic rubbish from beginning to end. What, after all, is a 'great possession'? A copy of the Gutenberg Bible might be so described and so might the autograph score of a Mozart quartet or a Holbein portrait. But to describe a modern watch, Japanese or otherwise, in such terms is ludicrous. Such a watch might be beautifully made, it might be a pleasant thing to own, but by no stretch of the imagination could it be called or 'ranked' 'one of the world's great possessions'. This being so, one would like to know who was responsible for the ranking, so that one could ask him, first, to set out his criteria and, second, to justify them. It is not impossible that he would find himself in some difficulty, should his anonymity ever be breached.

Real food
Food which has been subjected to a minimum of processing. *See also* NATURAL FOOD, HEALTH FOOD, and WHOLE. 'Real Food' is, for some unexplained reason, always completely vegetarian. Nuts, honey, fruit and vegetables are 'real food', fish and meat, no matter how fresh and however uncontaminated by additives and preservatives, are not. No harm is done, provided one realizes before going in what such a shop as Real Foods, 6 Cheap Street, Bath, will have in stock. For those in the know, 'Real Foods' is an acceptable shorthand, but for outsiders it could be confusing.

Regal
High style, grand. *The Dictionary of Diseased English* defined it as 'associated with royalty' and added 'always a popular and nostalgic concept in republics, such as Germany and the United States'. One should, with hindsight, have said 'republics, particularly the United States', in view of the growing passion for things royal, or supposedly royal, in that country. Having long since shown their king the door, the Americans are free to indulge in royal fantasies of a kind which frequently amaze the British and which constitute yet another psychological barrier between the two countries. The Palm Beach Polo and Country Club, for instance, advertises itself as 'the most regal resort community in American' (*New Yorker*, 20 Dec 1982). What exactly does this mean, or perhaps more to the point, what do Americans understand by it? In fairness, there are certainly many Americans who would find it amusing or absurd. They are for the most part those without the money, the temperament or the inclination to stay at the Palm Beach Polo and Country Club. The advertisement is not for them.

   But, for the serious-minded and those whose hearts are in the right place, 'regal' is a most alluring word, suggesting wealth, breeding, elegance, diamonds and leisure activities of the highest class. If an impresario can gather dozens of such people together in the same place at one time, the result is 'a regal resort community', which would bear remarkably little resemblance to such genuine regal resort communities as already exist, such as Brighton and Bognor Regis.

Relevant
Fashionable, socialist, left wing, in tune with today's society. 'Relevant' is a useful word, provided one specifies what the subject under discussion is relevant to. To say that someone or something is 'relevant', and t

leave the matter there, is like saying that a car is faster or a man is fatter. One must be given the other half of the story. Or so one would have thought. But today 'relevant' is increasingly used as an absolute and as a term of praise. To be 'relevant' is to be good, not to be 'relevant' is not only bad but downright dangerous and evil. One is not supposed to ask what 'relevant' means. One should know.

But, for those with faith, there can be problems. What, for instance, does a reviewer mean when he says of a novel 'Its ideas are strangely modern and relevant' (*New York Review of Books*, 3 Dec 1981)? Relevant to what? Possibly to today's society and its problems but, in that case, to which problems? It can hardly be relevant to all of them. Careful investigation and much discussion suggests that, for those who use the word in this way, 'relevant' is almost a synonym for 'modern'. If this is so, 'Its ideas are strangely modern and relevant' amounts to saying, 'Its ideas are strangely modern and modern', which seems hardly worth the extra printing cost.

The Chairman of the Further and Higher Education Committee of the Inner London Education Authority also seems to have been using 'relevant' to mean 'modern', when he referred to 'the recent and welcome evolution of the Scout movement into a more socially aware and relevant organisation' (*The Daily Telegraph*, 2 Dec 1982). In this case, however, 'more socially aware and relevant', taken as a block comment, undoubtedly meant, among other things, 'less right-wing', which would be included in the Chairman's definition of 'modern'.

Relocation package

Removal expenses. In today's industrial world, 'relocation packages' are always 'generous'. 'We offer a generous relocation package' (*The Daily Telegraph*, 11 Dec 1981) means, in simple English, 'We pay quite a high proportion of what it costs you to leave one house and install yourself in another'. Different firms interpret 'relocation package' in different ways and it is prudent to discover well in advance exactly how the phrase is being defined. Some employers will pay the total cost of selling one house and buying another, together with the actual removal charges, and others are prepared to meet only part of the whole bill. All, however, would certainly consider themselves 'generous'.

Re-manufactured

Rebuilt. For generations industrious and economical ladies have been ~npicking yesterday's garments and knitting them up again into some-
:ng more in line with today's fashion and, if one were short of a word to

S

Sales executive
Salesman, representative. Selling has never had the same prestige in the UK as it has in the USA and, in order to attract people of competence and intelligence to it various devices are employed to grade it up as an occupation. A favourite phrase at the present time is 'sales executive' but, although this may look and sound good, it can be extremely misleading. The company which announces that it requires 'additional Sales Executives in 1. Tyne Tees, 2. Kent, Surrey, Sussex' (*The Daily Telegraph*, 18 Feb 1982) is using the term very loosely indeed. An 'executive', if the word means anything at all, is a person who is engaged in some form of administration (see *The Dictionary of Diseased English* for a detailed discussion of this) and who, in most cases, is responsible for the work of other people. A sales manager might properly be described as a 'sales executive', but the people needed for Tyne Tees, Kent, Surrey and Sussex are salesmen, not sales managers. Those who apply for these jobs are consequently being defrauded.

Scotch
Aberdeen Angus. When a restaurant includes on its menu 'Roast Scotch Beef' (menu, Great Northern Hotel, London, July 1982) it is following a tradition, or rather myth, which encourages people to think that there is something very special about beef produced in Scotland. Scottish farmers do nothing to weaken the belief and have even fostered a myth within a myth, that the beef which comes from Aberdeen Angus cattle has no equal anywhere in the world. So all-powerful is this legend that it has become almost an article of faith in the meat and restaurant trades, where the motto for a long time has been 'Scotch beef is best and Aberdeen Angus is best of all'.

Most unfortunately for the fairytale, however, careful research has recently shown that the breed and the pedigree of beef cattle has nothing to do with the ultimate quality of the meat and that what really determines whether it is tender or not is the environment during the hours immediately before slaughter. If the animal is kept quietly before it meets its end, the meat will be tender and the taste will be acceptable. If it is jostled, driven about and generally maltreated, the meat will be inferior. So, for all it has to do with quality, 'Roast Scotch Beef' might just as well be 'Roast Essex Beef' or 'Roast Gloucestershire Beef'.

If the meat has to come from north of the Border, however, it is as well to get the adjective right. The people and their habits are 'Scottish', or 'Scots', the beef, for some reason, is always 'Scotch'. 'Charcoal grilled Scottish Rump Steak' (menu, Great Northern Hotel, London, July 1982) would mean 'Rump Steak cooked in the Scottish manner', whatever that might be.

Selection

A few. A commonly found piece of estate agents' rubbish. 'A selection of beautifully modernised flats' (agent's board outside a house in Sussex Gardens, London, seen on 25 Jan 1983). One understands the problem. Unless he is to have his board repeatedly repainted until all the flats have been sold, the agent cannot specify the number of flats he has to dispose of. Today, when the board goes up, it is 'Eight beautifully modernised flats', but tomorrow it could be seven and the day after, six. It is a ten green bottles situation. To say simply 'beautifully modernised flats' would not do, however, because this would not convey the correct message, 'Hurry, hurry, only one or two left'. 'A selection of' does the job very nicely. It keeps the number of flats continuously vague and, at the same time, gives the impression that the particular flats on sale have been carefully chosen from a larger number, which is, of course, quite untrue.

Select number

One or two, a few. *See also* LIMITED. This is a curious piece of Managementese, particularly common on the sales side of businesses, where English tends to be at its most diseased nowadays. One firm will say, 'We're now looking for a select number of Sales Management professionals' (*The Sunday Times*, 14 March 1982) and another has 'an immediate need to appoint a select number of ambitious men and women to train to become District Managers' (*The Daily Telegraph*, 26 Aug 1982). In cases like these, the company must have at least a rough idea of the number of people it wants, but it is reckoned to be important not to reveal this. The impression has to be given that the sifting of candidates will be extremely thorough and that only the very best will survive the process. 'Select number' carries out this task very well. It gives applicants the feeling that, should they be lucky, they will be not only 'selected' but 'select', and it leaves the employer free to explore the market and to take on as many or as few people as he pleases. The phrase is peculiar to this field. One could not, for example, go to a shop and ask for 'a select number of bananas'. The shopkeeper would want to know how many bananas one wanted. But there it is, apparently a difference between Sales Management professionals and bananas.

Self image

Self-respect, oneself as seen by the rest of the world. This strange expression, popular among psychologists and their hangers-on, is liable to leave anyone else baffled. How should one translate it in such a jargon-loaded context as 'The rewards can be meaningful and numerous in terms of total educational perspective, self image and future career goals' (*New York Times*, 27 Sept 1981)? In whose mind and perception is the image? If it is one's own mind, is the meaning 'oneself as one actually is', or 'oneself as one would like to be'? Is it, perhaps, a synonym for 'self-assessment' or 'self-analysis'? It is highly probable that one is not supposed to ask such awkward, unprofessional questions and that, by doing so, one has proved in advance that one could not benefit from the course.

Self-motivated

Able to work without constant supervision, naturally inclined to work hard. This expression has been with us long enough. Ten years ago it had a certain shock value, but now it is worn-out and used simply as ritual. There is no point in trying to dig below the surface in order to discover its meaning. 'The successful candidate will be self-motivated' (*The Birmingham Post*, 5 Nov 1981) might just as well be 'The successful candidate will be able to walk and have two ears' for all the meaning it has. It is interesting on such occasions to imagine someone looking into a mirror and asking himself, 'Am I self-motivated? Am I worthy?' This self-questioning has strong religious echoes, which is hardly surprising, since modern business is essentially a theology, and candidates for the management priesthood are quite properly required to look deeply into themselves and only to continue with their vocation if they can truthfully say that they 'have the experience, resilience and dependability and are self-motivated' (*The Sunday Times*, 25 Oct 1981). After this, 'will be capable of working unsupervised' (*Scotsman*, 7 Nov 1981) comes as a welcome gust of fresh air.

Self-shaming

Capable of making oneself ashamed? In trying to decide what a word or expression means, there are occasions when one has to admit defeat. 'Self-shaming' is such an expression. It now forms part of the novel-reviewer's regular bag of tools, especially in the USA, but what on earth is it trying to say? The context rarely helps, because that too is usually just as mystifying — 'Unflinchingly honest, self-shaming, humane and important' (*New Yorker*, 20 Sept 1982). All one can do is suggest possibilities which may turn out to be completely wrong. If a novel is 'self-shaming', who or what is the 'self'? Many novels should certainly be ashamed of themselves, but it would seem odd to publicize the fact. So the 'self' must be the readers, who could quite well be covered in shame for having bought or read such a rubbishy book. But this, too, seems unlikely, since the novel has already been praised for being 'unflinchingly honest, humane and important'. All one is left with is the thought that the writer leaves his readers with a sense of shame at how human beings can behave to one another, and maybe this is the message the reviewer intends to leave with us. His style of communication is, however, decidedly chancy, to say the least.

Self-starting

Able to work without being constantly kicked and prodded into action. The noun, 'self-starter', arrived earlier than the adjective and was thoroughly dealt with in *The Dictionary of Diseased English*. 'Self-starting' offers some slight relief from the ubiquitous and nearly senile 'self-starter' and fortunately its unintended comic possibilities are even greater. Technical representatives for a firm making industrial cleaning machines, for instance, are told that 'they will be ambitious, lively and self-starting' (*The Daily Telegraph*,f 12 Jan 1982). The two last qualifications raise them to the level of the machines they are employed to sell.

Sensibilities

Jaded nerves, irritations. This specialized meaning of the word has been gaining ground in the USA and it is as well to be forewarned, in case it should make an appearance here in the UK. It is usually found cocooned in such advertising poetry as 'Quiet tones and hushed beauty to soothe twentieth century sensibilities' (*New York Times*, 27 Sept 1981). The tones and beauty in this case belonged to carpets and it is, one supposes, just possible that the businessman, near to collapse after an appalling day, might become human again after looking at his carpet for a few minutes. The most interesting feature of this particular quotation, however, is the assumption that today's 'sensibilities' are undesirable ones, not those which result in the opening of the mind and soul to new and satisfying experiences.

Shirt-sleeves
Able and inclined to get down to the practical details of the job. *The Dictionary of Diseased English* dealt with 'short-sleeved', and here one need do little more than record the variant, 'shirt-sleeves'. It should perhaps be emphasized that the act of removing one's jacket at work and of facing colleagues and clients in one's shirt is purely symbolic. It does not indicate an immediate intention to carry out some form of manual work, merely that, in the best American fashion, one is ready and prepared to exert oneself to the full. With this in mind, an International Sales Manager is told 'Essentially you must be a "shirt-sleeves" individual' (*The Daily Telegraph*, 24 June 1982). The use of the inverted commas, in 1982, is interesting, indicating perhaps that the company is old-established, conservative and highly respected and that such phrases do not come naturally to it.

Significant amount
A great deal. 'Significant' is a coward's word, used to avoid revealing the full amount in all its horror. To be told by a prospective employer that 'these positions will involve a significant amount of travel' (*The Daily Telegraph*, 26 Aug 1982) is to invite the question, 'How much?', to which the wise applicant will make sure he gets an answer. 'Significant' is always an unsatisfactory adjective because what is significant to one person may not be to another. 'You are likely to be away from home for 200 nights in the year' might be a promise of paradise to some, but misery and deprivation to others.

Site
Factory. The 'site' used to be the ground on which a factory was built. Now, with the fashionable anxiety to avoid the obscene word 'factory' at any cost, it has come to mean the buildings themselves. One firm announces that it 'manufactures a wide range of pharmaceutical products at the purpose built site near Pontypool' (*The Daily Telegraph* 19 Feb 1982) and another explains that 'The positions report directly to the Site General Managers at key manufacturing centres' (*The Daily Telegraph*, 19 Feb 1982). But, if the site is now the factory, what, one may well ask, is the new word for what used to be the site? No alternative

seems to have appeared so far and until something is done to clear the matter up there are going to be people looking at the landscape and saying, 'What a splendid site for a site', which would not represent communication at its most elegant or most effective.

Situation

Four Managementese padding syllables, meaning nothing at all. 'Situation' is inserted, like the notorious four-letter word on a different kind of occasion, when the accompanying noun is felt to be insufficiently impressive to be allowed to stand alone. One recent example can be allowed to serve for all the rest. It refers to a telecommunications installation and the cautious, perhaps anxious, Top Man is made to ask, 'Is it sophisticated enough to handle all my message situations?' (*New Yorker*, 14 Sept 1981). The Bell Telephone Corporation naturally assures him that it is and the mini-drama comes to a happy ending. Simple people like ourselves, however, do not have 'message situations'. We have people trying to reach us on the telephone.

Skin fitness

Skin tone. 'Fitness', whether of the skin or any other part of the anatomy, is, like 'fit', vague and a rather silly term. One cannot be just 'fit'. One has to be fit for something. In everyday language, 'fit' usually means little more than 'not fat, and able to walk about and climb stairs without puffing and blowing'. 'Skin fitness' would seem to be something quite out of the ordinary. The body, after all, has quite a lot of skin. Is all of it to be brought to a state of 'fitness' or only some of it, possibly the skin of the face and neck? 'Skin fitness' is the new byword for looking good' (*The Times*, 5 Jan 1982) would suggest that what is being considered is the visible skin, but does that mean only the skin above the shoulders or are the hands and wrists included, too? In any case, what does one do in order to achieve 'skin fitness'? The answer, as one might have guessed, is not to make one's skin do exercises, but to go to the chemist and buy something expensive in a tube or pot.

Sleep technology

Beds and bedding. It had to come. One can no longer just lie down and go to sleep. Experts had to examine the whole process from beginning to end and then come up with beds designed from first principles, as if truly restful and efficient sleep had never existed before. This done, it became possible to promote 'the greatest advance in sleep technology in 40 years' (*New York Times*, 27 Sept 1981). This phenomenal achievement was not, as might have been supposed, a bed with built-in rocking mechanism or a mattress which released a mild dose of anesthetic every time one turned over, but a mere range of sofa-beds.

Smothered
Hidden under a thick covering. This is hardly the most elegant of restaurant terms and there are those who would find it repulsive. But where it is used it is clearly intended to pull customers in, not send them away. 'A heap of freshly baked pork ribs, smothered in delicious barbeque (*sic*) sauce', promises the menu of the Tennessee Pancake House (Leicester Square, London, July 1982). The Tennessee Pancake House is not the Savoy or the Ritz and it very sensibly provides what it has reason to believe its customers like, which is probably what the staff like, too. If people are fond of barbecue sauce, then let us give them plenty of it, the philosophy probably runs. If a little is good, then a lot must be even better, so they shall have their pork ribs *smothered* in the stuff, much as children like to have their pudding *smothered* in custard or chocolate sauce. But there is always the possibility that things may not turn out exactly as the menu suggests. 'Smothered' is, after all, not a precise term and, when the dish arrives, there may not be as thick a coating of sauce as one expected. Worse still, the sauce may be there for a purpose. It could turn out to be more interesting than the pork ribs underneath.

So-called
Bogus, pretending to be. 'So-called' has become a difficult word to use with any great degree of precision. The Germans are at the root of the problem. When a German uses '*sogennant*', he means 'as it is called', with no suggestion that it should not really be called anything of the sort and that to do so constitutes arrogance and fraud. The English usage is quite different. A 'so-called policeman' would mean the man was not really a policeman at all, and a 'so-called bargain' would be no bargain. In the USA, however, with its large number of German immigrants, the two traditions have become mixed and confused, so that it is often far from easy to decide which meaning is intended. An illustration of the dilemma is provided by 'so-called consumer legislation directed at the testing industry' (*American Psychologist*, March 1981). Is the writer simply drawing attention for the benefit of the innocent to the fact that there is something known as 'consumer legislation' or is he pooh-poohing the whole idea of such legislation? One suspects the latter, but it is impossible to be sure.

Software

Printed material — books, pamphlets, instruction manuals, question-naires, anything on paper. It is humbling to realize that in this computer age books are now simply software. However, times change and one must not stand in the way of either software or hardware. It is possible, even so, to wish that our new technologists would learn to express themselves a little more elegantly and would realise that in English one cannot glue noun to noun ad infinitum without running the risk of being misunderstood. 'Assisting in the development of audit interrogation software' (*The Daily Telegraph*, 11 Dec 1981) would sound splendid in German, but it has the poor English standing on their heads wondering which noun goes with what.

Sophisticated

Elegant? Modern? Full of the latest devices? One person's guess is as good as another's, confronted with a piece of nonsense like 'the opportunity to move into a sophisticated environment in one of the City's newest offices' (*The Daily Telegraph*, 6 Jan 1982). It is nice to know that such an opportunity exists, but what exactly is 'a sophisticated environment'? One can only suggest some of the possible ingredients. It would look expensive and the furniture could well have been designed and made specially. There would be a lot of pot plants around, supplied and maintained under contract. Telephone equipment and typewriters would be of the latest type. Soundproofing and double glazing would keep the traffic roar at bay. Colour schemes would be carefully thought out and pleasant. If there did happen to be any pictures on the walls, they would be expensive prints. It would be interesting to visit the place, to discover if these guesses were correct.

Sophistication

Knowledge of, acquaintance with, judgement of. This is apparently a new sense of the word, to be found in, for example, 'They perceive a lack of confidence in their sophistication with national issues' (*American Journal of Psychiatry*, 12 Dec 1981). *The Dictionary of Diseased English* defined 'sophistication' as 'the state of being sophisticated, highly developed, highly trained and educated, highly cultured'. This was, of course, a gallant attempt to make the best of a bad job, since 'sophistication' has long passed the point of having any agreed meaning at all. But to talk of a person's 'sophistication with' anything is to enter a world in which linguistic tradition has disappeared up the chimney and syntax is anything one wishes. In the example quoted above, the *Ameri-*

can Journal of Psychiatry is probably trying to say something like, 'their assessment of national issues', but its professional vocabulary has unfortunately got in the way.

Sourcing

Discovering suitable or the best suppliers. This is a technical term used in the clothing trade and, as such, there can be no objection to it. Everyone in the trade knows what is meant and it is of no importance if the general public is puzzled. So one accepts without reservation 'the person appointed will be responsible for sourcing grey cloth' (*The Daily Telegraph*, 17 Sept 1981), and 'You should have clothing marketing experience, including sourcing' (*The Daily Telegraph*, 17 Sept 1981). There are, however, signs that 'sourcing' may be on the way to becoming a word in more general use. One student was overheard saying to another on the London Underground (12 Dec 1982), 'I'm having a bit of trouble with the sourcing', and what that meant is guesswork. It is most unlikely that he was engaged in cloth-buying in his spare time and the probability is that ten years ago he would have said, 'I'm having a bit of trouble with my source material', or 'I'm having a bit of trouble finding the sources of these references'. There is, of course, a considerable difference between the two, which makes one think that it would be a good thing to discourage 'sourcing' while there is yet time.

Spearhead

Lead, push forward. This is one of those aggressive, attacking metaphors which modern management loves so much. It is frequently applied to the most prosaic of operations, presumably to add a little excitement to the lives of those who have to engage in them. 'A Landfill Development Manager', for instance, is required, 'to help spearhead the programme of landfill acquisitions' (*The Daily Telegraph*, 8 June 1982). Now, 'landfill' is 'tipping' and this man's job includes finding sites where unwanted material can be tipped. It is not a romantic task and one can only hope that the use of such a warlike word as 'spearhead' does not encourage expectations which cannot be met.

Specially

Properly? Suitably? 'Half a chicken, specially seasoned' (menu, Myllet Arms, Perivale, Middlesex, England, July 1982). The word certainly makes one think and possibly marvel. Cooks and even chefs are in the habit of seasoning their dishes, even if this means no more than adding salt to the cooking water. But it is not normal and indeed distinctly vulgar to make any mention of this on the menu. A cookery book is one thing, a menu quite another. But what, in any case, is one supposed to understand by 'specially seasoned'? Seasoned with what? With some seasoning particularly appropriate to half a chicken? Specially seasoned for you, sir, and for you, madam? In default of other evidence, it would be safest to assume that one was simply getting half a chicken and that the anonymous special seasoning, if present, would not make a great deal of difference one way or another.

Spokesperson

Spokesman. It is no doubt a good thing to tilt the organization of society a little more in favour of women, perhaps a lot more, but some of the methods aimed at achieving this have produced more mirth than equality. The replacement of 'man' by 'person' on all possible occasions is such a method. We have not yet reached 'personkind', but it will certainly come. Meanwhile, the ultra-feminists, who are not overgifted with a sense of humour, count 'chairperson' and 'spokesperson' as two of their major successes and they are liable to jump with great ferocity on anyone who refers to a woman as a 'spokesman' or 'chairman'. The correct usage now is indicated by 'THPA spokesperson, Mrs Heather Harding' (*Daily Express*, 11 Feb 1982). It is only fair to point out that there are many women who detest these new titles and find them ludicrous, which indeed they are. To unbelievers, a 'chairperson' is quite likely to suggest someone who hires out deckchairs or takes the money for them and there are similar dangers elsewhere.

State-of-the-art

The most up-to-date and consequently the best. First applied to hi-fi equipment in the 1970s, it has now spread to everything. The origins of this dreadful expression are obscure, but they were certainly in the USA, where there may possibly be some link with the annual State of the Union Message. The success of 'state-of-the-art' has been extraordinary. There is almost nothing to which it has not been applied at one time or another. The business world took to it immediately. One firm has 'a new 4341 computer which makes our MIS Department competitively state of the art' (*Boston Globe*, 11 Oct 1981), another says it is able 'to produce innovative solutions to complex communications problems by employing state-of-the-art techniques' (*Sunday Telegraph*, 29 Nov 1981), and a third emphasizes the new service it can offer its customers 'involving state-of-the-art computer and communications technology' (*The Daily Telegraph*, 4 Feb 1982). British Nuclear Fuels 'has made a major investment in State-of-the-Art hardware and software' (*The Daily Telegraph*, 4 Feb 1982), flats are offered in New York 'featuring state-of-the-art security and ultra-modern kitchens' (*New Yorker*, 19 Oct 1981) — one wonders why it was not 'state-of-the-art kitchens' — and, still in New York, the new recruit is assured that he will be 'working alongside a high-powered team of skilled professionals in a fast-paced state-of-the-art environment' (*New York Times*, 27 Sept 1981).

How the world managed in the primitive days before life became state-of-the-art is almost impossible to imagine.

Steely

Hard, firm, tasting of iron filings? An in-word with little to say to the outside world and therefore almost impossible to define. One knows and feels when something is 'steely', one cannot be expected to be able to communicate the sensation in mere words, a situation which makes life difficult for anyone who is trying to learn. The matter under discussion may be 'dry or at least dryish white wines, often characterised by an underlying firm, cool, steely style' (*The Times*, 31 Oct 1981) or music, where one could refer to 'the steely adroitness of Victoria Postinokova in dispensing the solo piano part' (*The Times*, 30 Oct 1981). While recognizing the great difficulty of finding words to describe sensations, 'steely' does seem to present the reader with particularly severe problems. If both the music and the wine experts of *The Times* use 'steely' on consecutive days, one could be forgiven for suspecting that a fashion for 'steely' was sweeping through the building at that time, to be replaced by another in-word in due course.

Strong character

Person with ideas of his own. This expression has been gradually creeping into Managementese over the past two or three years and it now possesses enough nuisance value to justify a mention here. There is nothing necessarily wrong with a person of strong character, although he can be difficult to live with. The essence of such an individual is that he believes firmly in the rightness of what he is doing and that he is unwilling to compromise in the pursuit of his ends, however stupid or misguided these may be. People of this type have existed in all ages and in societies less tolerant than our own in the UK today. A fair proportion of them have landed up in prison or at the stake.

With this as background, one should look very carefully at such sentences as 'We are looking for candidates who can play a leading role in a team of strong characters' (*The Sunday Times*, 25 Oct 1981). What this almost certainly means is the team, a research team, contains a number of bright people whom, despite their disinclination to conform to the usual rules, the company is anxious to hold on to, since they are producing commercially useful ideas. An industrial concern cannot say publicly that it employs awkward customers. 'Strong characters' is more acceptable, although it means exactly the same thing.

Substance

Drugs. This very genteel and clinical-sounding euphemism, recently introduced in the USA, is not yet widely known or used on this side of the Atlantic and advance warning may be helpful, in case any unfortunate misunderstanding should occur. It is to be found in such contexts as 'Special programs in Alcohol and Substance Abuse' (*New Yorker*, 29 June 1981). These particular 'programs' are available in a psychiatric hospital in Vermont, but similar opportunities exist in many other places, since today's society unfortunately contains so many alcoholics and drug addicts. 'Substance abuse' is certainly ingenious. Not even the most socially exalted addict would find it offensive and his relatives could even refer to it with some pride.

Substantial

Large. This is a perfect word for a society which, except in sexual matters, is increasingly frightened of calling a spade a spade. A company draws back from saying it is 'large' or 'big', because someone else might claim to be bigger and, in any case, these simple monosyllables would be considered vulgar nowadays. 'Substantial' keeps the size pleasantly vague and conveys the idea of solidity as a bonus. Solicitors, accountants and banks, with their 'substantial clients', have known the value of the word for many years. Industry has been rather slow in realizing its possibilities, but it is catching up fast.

So one comes across 'a substantial organisation, with a £ multi-million turnover' (*The Daily Telegraph*, 2 June 1982), and the South African engineering concern 'with substantial procurement of components and assemblies from sub-contractors' (*Sunday Telegraph*, 22 Nove 1981). A company in the Midlands 'is engaged on a substantial development programme' (*The Birmingham Post*, 5 Nov 1981) and in Wiltshire an estate agent offers 'a substantial Queen Anne country house, 4 reception, 8 beds' (*Sunday Telegraph*, 15 Nov 1981). 'Substantial' is an important item in the house agent's stock-in-trade. It avoids saying that a house is 'large', which would make it more difficult to sell, and at the same time it conveys the helpful idea that the place is solid and well built.

'Substantial' is also much prized by academics and literary critics. It allows one to say, in effect, that a book or an article is not just words, but it also provides a handy opportunity for caution, since one does not have to give any precise information about its meatiness. Nobody could be offended by being told publicly that 'He provides a substantial introduction to current literary trends' (*New York Review of Books*, 3 Dec 1981).

Substitute

Synthetic? Clever chemists have discovered substitutes for a great range of natural products but in describing them it is necessary to distinguish between those products which are actually substitutes, that is, different substances which perform the same function as the original, and those which produce by artificial means something which is chemically and physically indistinguishable, or nearly so, from what is found in nature. The two are sometimes confused in a way likely to result in general bewilderment. 'Processes for the production of substitute natural gas' (*The Daily Telegraph*, 1 July 1982) is a case in point.

Substrate

Basis, cause. A pompous and idiotic attempt to blind the reader with science and Latinity, very popular, as one might have suspected, among the social scientists and psychiatrists whose wares are always in need of being dressed up. 'The attempt to specify further the psychobiological substrate of psychiatric illnesses' (mailing by Baywood Publishing Co., New York, Sept 1981) is a rather choice example.

Superior

Higher quality. To decide if, in a particular context, this long-suffering word means anything at all, one only has to ask, 'Superior to what?' If the sentence collapses as a result, so much the better. 'Born of superior ingredients', says an advertisement for Smirnoff Vodka (*New Yorker*, 19 Oct 1981). Superior to the ingredients used for other brands of vodka? If so, what are these ingredients and in what way are they superior to the rye and potatoes the Russians have used for generations? And the house 'with superior views over the Firth of Forth' (*Edinburgh Evening News*, 6 Nov 1981). Are these views 'superior' because the house is higher up than its neighbours or superior in kind? If the latter is the case, in what way are they 'superior'? Do they contain, perhaps, finer and more golden sunsets, more sea, nicer trees, fewer ugly buildings, or what? One might as well know, because the views are clearly included in the price.

Sympathetically modernized

Not vandalized, modernized without ruining a pleasant old building. This estate agents' word is applied to properties which are well above the middle of the price range, but not to those at the top, or nearly so. Houses below the 'sympathetically' line are 'tastefully modernized', those above it 'sensitively modernized', which is another way of saying that good architects cost money. Gloucester Square, London W2, is grade two and so, inevitably, one finds 'The properties have been sympathetically modernised' (advertisement by Chestertons, *London Portrait*, Jan 1983). *See also* TASTEFULLY.

T

Tastefully
In a manner approved and popularized by the women's magazines. Those with taste never mention it, those without it talk of little else. Since house agents have no taste whatever — they cannot afford such a luxury — they are among the word's best customers, always happy to promote the 'tastefully modernised old semi-detached cottage' (*Western Gazette*, June 1982). For something slightly more up-market, the phrase would be SYMPATHETICALLY MODERNIZED and, close to the top, 'sensitively modernized.'

Tastemaker
Person who influences the taste of others, who determines their taste for them. The existence of the profession of tastemaking in addition to that of opinion-forming is a depressing thought, but there can no longer be any doubt about its reality, faced with an advertisement for 'an international tastemaker's fresh ideas for decorating, entertaining, week-ending, gift giving, table setting, collecting and more' (*New Yorker*, 28 Sept 1981). These new experts have been brought into being by the desperate anxiety of so many bored women with more money than sense to do what the best people are doing. With no confidence in their own judgement, they have come to rely absolutely on someone else doing their thinking and deciding for them. In such a situation the all-round tastemaker could hardly fail to do well. He is the modern Beau Nash, able to impose his rules of behaviour on all-too-willing victims. Yet his function is not quite what the name might suggest. He does not originate 'taste'. He observes trends in international high society and, for a suitable fee, passes them on to people without direct access to such society. He is a 'taste intermediary', a 'taste pimp', rather than a 'taste-maker'.

Tasty
Tasting of something. Nowadays, when so much food tastes of nothing

at all, a good selling trick is to label this or that as 'tasty'. What it tastes of is not particularly important. The strength, not the quality, of the taste is what matters. A restaurant can therefore offer with every confidence, 'Two tasty sausages' (menu, Myllet Arms, Perivale, Middlesex, England, July 1982). Few of its customers will remember what the menu said while they are actually eating the sausages. 'Tasty' was the word which clinched the order.

'Tasty' cheese is another matter. The adjective is applied only to Cheddar cheese and, with rare exceptions, it is used only by people below the line which divides the upper from the lower middle class. Above that line, one says 'strong' or 'mature'. Fortnum and Mason and Harrods offer 'mature' Cheddar, not 'tasty' Cheddar.

Thermal
Warm. There have been thermos flasks for generations, so even the most ignorant and stupid should be aware that 'thermos' has something to do with heat. The adjective 'thermal', however, has been part of the popular vocabulary only a comparatively short time. It is used especially in connection with clothing. 'Warm clothes' have become unfashionable. They are associated with children, chilblains, and grandparents. 'Thermal' clothes are quite another matter. Nothing could be more modern, more desirable, and more worth paying a lot of money for. It is this last virtue which has made 'thermal' so popular with the advertisers. So one can now buy a 'fleecy lined thermal jacket from only £9.95' (*Daily Express*, 30 Dec 1982) and, by choosing one's materials and maker carefully, avoid 'the clammy feeling associated with many items of thermal clothing' (brochure by Gordale Co., Bingley, Yorkshire, England, Dec 1982).

Warm clothing, indeed, is such a novelty now that the Wool Marketing Board itself has found it necessary to publicize wool as 'Wool — the original thermal fibre' (leaflet, *How to be warm this winter*, 1982). The pendulum is bound to swing eventually and, when it does, we shall find 'warm jackets' and 'warm socks' selling like hot cakes. Meanwhile, one should protect oneself against exploitation and overcharging by reminding oneself that between 'thermal' and 'warm' there is absolutely no difference.

Timber-based operation
A timber-yard. Every form of commercial undertaking must undergo the full grading-up treatment nowadays, if it is to remain in business. So a 'timber-yard', which is as solid and respectable a business as one is

likely to find, has to be veneered over to become something more distinguished. It will, of course, require a different breed of manager, so that one advertises for 'someone to head an established timber-based operation' (*The Daily Telegraph*, 10 Dec 1981). This suggests a splendid range of possibilities. 'A grass-based operation' might be a football club, 'a road-based operation' a haulage business, and 'a flour-based operation' a bakery. And these are only examples.

Thick cream
Cream. *See* DOUBLE CREAM. 'Cool thick cream' (menu, Myllet Arms, Perivale, Middlesex, England, July 1982). There is no difference between 'thick cream' and 'double cream'. Both are what used to be called 'cream'. By removing some, but not all of the fat, it is possible to produce a much more watery liquid called 'coffee cream', which is so close to milk that few would notice the difference.

Totally
Very. 'Totally' is a word which needs to be used with discrimination. It is possible for something to be 'totally dry', that is, to contain no measurable moisture at all, 'totally deaf', or 'totally penniless', but most other uses of the word are exaggerations. Even a 'totally exhausted' person can open and shut his eyes and waggle a finger. But the advertisers live by exaggeration and find 'totally' much to their taste. They have no misgivings about describing a knitted dress as 'totally luxurious, totally today' (*New Yorker*, 28 Sept 1981). Asked for the difference between 'luxurious' and 'totally luxurious', they would probably answer that, if the fashion trade depended on logic and precision, it would have died long ago. *See also* LUXURIOUS.

Toward, towards
This cannot be defined, because, in academic circles, where it belongs, it has no lexical meaning. It is used, in the titles of learned papers and theses, in order to safeguard the author from pin-pricking criticism. 'The Importance of the Comma in Act One of *Macbeth*' would be far too dangerous, because some minute fault in scholarship might be detected by those who make it their business to look for such things and to castigate the culprit. If, however, one adds the all-important word 'Toward' or 'Towards' — Towards a Theory of the Importance of the Comma, &c' — then safety is at hand, because one is moving in the direction of a theory or conclusion but has not yet committed oneself to it.

There is consequently an abundance of such titles as 'Toward a Contextual Approach to Prehistoric Change' (catalogue, Academic Press, New York 1982). It is a cowardly trick and no-one should be deceived by it.

Town house

A house in one of the better parts of London or, much less frequently, one of the more agreeable provincial places, such as Salisbury or Edinburgh. Millions of people live in towns, but very few of them enjoy the prestige and amenities of a town house. This curious expression had its origins in the days when well-to-do people maintained one house in the country and one in London. House agents preserve the fiction of such a life, because so many of their more profitable customers enjoy daydreaming that they are living before World War I and that they are richer and more exalted than is in fact the case. The language with which to get them on the hook is 'Close to Belgrave Square, a spacious Town House of the utmost merit' (*Country Life*, 21 May 1981). The capital letters are very important. *See* CAPITALS, USE OF.

Track record

Career, experience, record. As *The Dictionary of Diseased English* pointed out, 'track record' has almost replaced the traditional terms, no doubt because of its associations with athletics, record-breaking, and the defeat of all competition. All that one can do now is to point out, with sincere regrets, that the expression has now greatly widened its field of application and that its stamina appears to be undiminished. In the 1970s, the expression nearly always referred to people. It is still extensively used in this way — 'He must already have had similar experience, preferably overseas/Middle East with proven track record' (*Sunday Telegraph*, 3 Jan 1982) — but nowadays the firm or some part of it is even more likely to emphasize its 'track record'. 'We are an aggressive marketing oriented company with excellent track record' (*New York Times* 27 Sept 1981) is how one firm throws out its chest, while an educational establishment, anxious to push its Operational Research course, tells prospective students that it is 'a vital function with an impressive track record' (*The Sunday Times*, 28 Feb 1982). Ten years from now 'track record' will probably have disappeared and some other equally brilliant and striking metaphor will have taken its place. It is interesting to wonder what this will be. 'Flight path', perhaps, or 'orbit'.

Trading orientated
With retailing experience. One's 'orientation' is one's training and experience, the direction in which fate has turned one's nose. Since everyone is anxious to be as 'professional' as his neighbours and rivals, it is important to use the correct terminology at all times. For this reason, a firm which sells building materials will demand, not that its new managing director shall have had a successful career in some branch of retailing, but that he 'must be trading orientated' (*The Daily Telegraph*, 7 Jan 1982). One can only hope that the right man understands the language.

Translucent flames
Energy which is not showy or vulgar? Music critics may realise immediately what is meant by 'the strong translucent flames of the BBC Symphony Orchestra at the end' (*The Times*, 30 Oct 1980), but a mere music lover could well find such poetry puzzling. One gathers, however, that something exciting was taking place and perhaps that is as far as communication can reasonably be expected to go.

Trim
Neat, not flamboyant. One understands without difficulty how a woman or her clothers can be 'trim', but it requires a considerable effort of the imagination to transfer the meaning to wine. Yet it is clear that one must do one's best, since wine writers are liable at any minute to tell the public that a particular wine 'retains its crisp, trim style' (*The Times*, 31 Oct 1981) and no-one wishes to be thought ignorant.

True professional
Devoted to the job, with a lifetime's experience. This strange expression is widely used to describe salesmen, but is rarely found in any other connection. Many people drift in and out of selling in the course of a lifetime. These are a lower breed, not to be confused with the True Professionals. Any other occupation has its professionals, but only selling can boast its True Professionals and they, in general, are the only people in which a reputable firm is interested nowadays. 'True Professionals with preferably a recognised structured Training programme geared to the retail trade are the people we want to talk to' (*The Daily Telegraph*, 18 Feb 1982) says one such firm, and it speaks for the rest.

U

Ultimate

The very best, the last word in. The difficulty with this word is that, if the ultimate is reached today, there is nothing left for tomorrow and all progress is blocked. *The Dictionary of Diseased English* produced and commented on some choice examples of this grossly over-used word, but its popularity seems undiminished by the passing of time. The real objection to 'ultimate' is that it encourages mental laziness on the part of both the user and the reader. It is a press-button word, guaranteed to produce automatic longing and approval. Nothing as old-fashioned as meaning is involved.

A few recent examples make this clear. A shipping line offers 'the ultimate cruise experience' (*Sunday Telegraph*, 24 Jan 1982). Interpreted logically, this could mean only the sinking of the ship and the death by drowning of everyone on board, but it seems unlikely that the cruise operator had exactly this in mind. So, too, with 'Macanudo. The ultimate cigar' (*New Yorker*, 14 June 1982) which should mean 'the last cigar you will smoke or ever want to', and 'the ultimate travel companion' (*New Yorker*, 31 May 1982), 'positively the last person you will ever travel with'.

'The deep dark ultimate in rich rum taste' (*New Yorker*, 5 Oct 1981) is more subtle and more difficult. Does this mean 'the darkest taste in rum one could possibly find' and, if so, what is a dark taste? Or is it 'the very rummiest of rum taste', and what does that mean? Rum can hardly taste of anything other than rum, unless something is seriously wrong with it. It is possibly the associations of rum, rather than the rum itself which the advertisement is thinking of, the deep, unquenchable passions of dusky West Indian ladies.

The person who is 'seeking the ultimate in furniture' (*New Yorker*, 14 Sept 1981) is likely to be disappointed, since the last piece of furniture has not yet been made and one might well have to wait a long time for it. But the search could help to relieve boredom.

Ultra-contemporary

In the latest style, STATE-OF-THE-ART. *The Dictionary of Diseased English* had 'ultra-modern', which it defined as 'in an uncompromisingly modern style', but not 'ultra-contemporary', which has appeared on the scene more recently. It is not easy at first sight to understand in what way 'ultra-contemporary' is different from 'ultra-modern', and the context is rarely of any help. A firm selling kitchen furniture, for example, will offer 'over sixty styles, from ultra-contemporary to the richest traditional' (*New York Times*, 27 Sept 1981). One knows well enough what 'the richest traditional' will look like. 'Richest', in American terms, means stained to a dark walnut colour and 'traditional' is imitation Colonial. So much is clear, but what is one to expect from 'ultra-contemporary'? The answer, alas, is exactly the same as from 'modern', 'ultra-modern' and 'contemporary' — plenty of formica, completely plain surfaces, with no mouldings or carvings to catch the dust, and with strong suggestions of the cook's galley on a large and expensive yacht.

Uncompromising

Not likely to compromise one? This is an unusual meaning of 'uncompromising' and it may not be what the author intended. But what alternatives could one suggest, where the advertisement is for an expensive perfume for men and says that it is 'Virile. Discreet. Refreshing. Uncompromising' (*New Yorker*, 14 June 1982)? Men indulging themselves in this way would probably be anxious not to be considered homosexual. They would not wish to be 'compromised' by the perfume, so it has to be 'uncompromising', in the sense of 'uncompromisingly masculine', whatever that may imply. The whole business is undoubtedly very subtle and, for those who are outside the world of male perfumes, very puzzling.

Understatement

Something simple, plain, unfussy. A 'statement', in the jargon employed in the furnishing and dress worlds, is a style which says to the world, 'This is me'. If one makes the point too strongly, one is guilty of 'overstatement', that is, flamboyance and perhaps vulgarity 'Understatement', on the other hand, is a form of presenting one's taste which relies on quietness and restraint. A furniture manufacturer, for example, can offer 'understatement in select cherry for town or country' (*New York Times*, 27 Sept 1981). By this he means plain surfaces, without mouldings, carvings or bizarre shapes, and simple fittings, with no mock-Germanic brassware. 'Understatement', in short, represents the antithesis of 'nouveau riche'. It is the style adopted by people who feel no need to flaunt their money and, for this reason, it is very rare.

Unique

Remarkable. As *The Dictionary of Diseased English* took pains to point out, to describe something as 'unique' means that it can be found only in one example. Every human being, for instance, is 'unique'. But the advertisers refuse to agree. Used as they use it, 'unique' is a hot property and they have no intention of allowing it to be mishandled by mere intellectuals. So an English restaurant will tell the world about its 'unique claret selection' (*The Birmingham Post*, 5 Nov 1981) — the good choice of Bordeaux available to the customer — an Australian hotel will refer to 'the semi-circle facade of its unique building' (brochure of the Wentworth Hotel, Sydney 1982) — its architecturally interesting building — and a refreshment place in New York will describe itself as 'New York's first and most unique outdoor café' (*New Yorker*, 5 July 1982) — that is, its most interesting and stylish outdoor café.

'Most unique' is by no means confined to the USA. A house in Sloane Square, London, for example, is put on the market as 'A most unique and easy to maintain low built house' (advertisement by George Trollope, *London Property*, mid-Jan 1983), which means that there is nothing like it in Sloane Square, where the houses tend to be on the tall side. With a little practice, it is not too difficult to read between the lines. At a holiday centre in Tanzania, 'The lodges and hotels are architecturally unique' (Wings brochure *Faraway Holidays*, Summer 1983) means, to those who have learnt the language, that the outside of these buildings is the most interesting thing about them, and that nothing remarkable is to be expected inside.

Faced with the task of selling some particularly bizarre or outrageous building, house agents will often fall back on 'unique' as the only truthful, yet flattering, term at their disposal and sing the praises of 'this quite unique modern property' (*Country Life*, 21 May 1981). Reviewers, searching around for an impressive-sounding word which will allow them to preserve such integrity as they possess and yet not interfere with the sales of the book, are equally grateful to have 'unique' in reserve. All kinds of book can qualify for such descriptions as 'Hardy's absolutely unique perspective' (*New York Review of Books*, 3 Dec 1981) and, of a particularly dull and uninspiring book, 'This unique study of the sense of self' (*New York Review of Books*, 3 Dec 1981). 'Unique' is indeed a word for all seasons.'

Unmatched

Impressive. Very few things or people could possibly be described as 'unmatched', which can only mean 'without equal'. But the minds of reviewers and critics do not, apparently, see the matter in quite this way. Oppressed by the sheer number of books with which they are required to deal, and by the less than brilliant quality of most of them, these hard-pressed people are always in the market for adjectives appropriate to their trade. 'Unmatched' is one of them. It is unlikely to annoy either an author or his publisher and few people will take the trouble to enquire too closely into its meaning. So sentences like 'Wilber's breadth of knowledge and thinking is unmatched' (*New York Review of Books*, 3 Dec 1981) go unchallenged and the reviewer draws his fee with a clear conscience.

Unsocial hours

Any hours not within the limits of Monday to Friday, 8 am to 6 pm. During the 1950s, the British trade unions created the marvellous fiction that there were normal, natural and God-given hours and days during which a man should work and that any labour performed outside these hours should be paid for at increased rates, if indeed it was right and proper for a person to oblige his employer in such a fashion. Since a dignified label was required for these grace-and-favour periods, the phrase 'unsocial hours' was invented by someone possessing a talent amounting to genius in these matters. Translated into more easily intelligible language, 'unsocial hours' are those during which a man, untrammelled by such trivial and annoying matters as employment, would normally and rightly be acting socially, drinking, playing darts or slumped asleep in front of a television screen. This is the background to the shipping company's advertisement for someone 'willing to work certain unsocial hours on voyage repairs' (*The Daily Telegraph*, 1 Dec 1981).

Urgent

Urging one on. This slightly unusual sense of 'urgent' has now entered the industrial field and it is as well to be aware of it, in case misunderstanding should occur. When found, it will be in this kind of context, 'You will be articulate, possessing an urgent sense of self-discipline' (*The Daily Telegraph*, 4 Feb 1982). Those who are accustomed to using 'urgent' in the traditional way might find this sentence somewhat perplexing.

Usage

Business. The semi-literate, such as sports reporters and businessmen, have a terror of repetition. They will go to extreme and often ludicrous lengths to find alternative expressions for some simple word, so that 'score', 'price' and the like do not appear twice in the same paragraph. They must be publicly seen to possess a rich vocabulary, even if that vocabulary behaves in a strange way. British Telecom, for instance, is an organization less happy with the English language than with electronics. For its Prestel service, it requires what it calls, somewhat flatteringly and with capital letters to emphasize the flattery, 'Account Executives'. These people earn a living 'both by bringing on (*sic*) substantial new business and by increasing the usage of existing customers' (*The Daily Telegraph*, 6 Jan 1982). What it presumably means by this far from happy sentence is that the Account Executives are required to obtain new customers and to persuade existing customers to make more use of the service. 'Usage of', in other words, means 'business from', but in his frantic efforts to avoid using 'business' again, the writer has got himself seriously lost. To 'increase the usage of existing customers' would be gradually to wear them out and this was probably not British Telecom's intention.

Utilise

Use. 'Never use a short word when a long one will do' is the golden rule among scientific people and their satellites and parasites. Those who are not aware of this are liable to waste a great deal of time looking for shades of meaning which do not in fact exist. They may, for example, believe that there must be some important difference between 'clinical methods utilised in professional practice' (*New York Times*, 27 Sept 1982) and 'clinical methods used in professional practice'. There are none, but the customer will have to pay more for the first than the second.

V

Vendor assurance
Setting customers' minds at rest. This remarkable phrase belongs particularly to the packaging world and, for those who are not used to it, it is liable to give rise to misunderstanding. A petfood concern, for example, is looking for someone to work on the improvement of its packaging systems. 'This,' it says, 'calls for an understanding not only of the importance of quality specifications, vendor assurance and test methodology', and then goes on to list what else is required of this paragon. 'Quality specifications' and 'test methodology' cause no problems, but 'vendor assurance' is a difficult one. The 'vendor' in this case is not the petfood company itself, but the shop which sells its products, and it is not the petfood people who need to be assured about their vendors, which 'vendor assurance' could well mean, but the vendors who must be given confidence that the cans will not leak or burst or the packets split. 'Vendor assurance' is one of those over-compressed phrases which would benefit from an extra word or two.

Very top
The most exalted, than whom none higher. 'Very top' is a good illustration of the danger of asking too much of a word. For some years, one got along very well with 'top executives'. These, as the phrase implies, were the people at the top of a business, the all-powerful figures who ran it. After a while, however, 'top executives' found itself in the same situation as the 'luxury coach' and 'luxury flat'. It became the norm, so that something better had to be found for those who really were the top men and the only possibility was to call them 'very top', more top than top, so to speak. Once that point had been reached, there had to be a completely new word to describe the next generation of these wonder-people and one waits for it with some apprehension.

Vibrant
Throbbing with life, exciting. Anything is allowed to be 'vibrant' now-

● **Victim blaming**

…adays. 'A beautiful vibrant city' (brochure of Wentworth Hotel, Sydney, Australia, 1982) reflects the truth to a certain extent, although visitors to Sydney are more likely, perhaps, to notice the traffic noise than the city's heartbeats. One could hardly miss the pulsations, however, on a cruise which offers 'vibrant nights of music and dance'(advertisement by Royal Viking Line, *London Portrait*, Jan 1983). it is necessary to make sure that advertisements like these do not fall into the wrong hands, since there may be those contemplating a visit to Australia or a couple of weeks' rest at sea who would not relish the thought of all this vibrancy or vibration. Not everyone enjoys being shaken for long periods.

Victim blaming

Blaming victims? Blaming oneself for being a victim? Victims blaming other people for allowing them to be victims? This social science word really can lead to immense confusion and there would be good reason to campaign for its speedy abolition. When, for example, one is encouraged to buy a book whose great merit is supposed to be that of 'suggesting environmental and structural changes as alternatives to victim blaming strategies' (mailing by Baywood Publishing Company, Farmingdale, New York, 1981), what is one supposed to understand? Three possibilities have been suggested above, but they could all be wrong. There must be a better way of doing the job, assuming that the job is communication.

Villa

Any structure rented for self-catering holiday purposes in a country bordering the Mediterranean. Broadly speaking, there are no 'villas' north of Paris and none at all in the UK. This is a highly specialized use of the word and anyone who thinks that, if he takes what he thinks of as a villa for a couple of weeks, he is going to get anything resembling a British surburban villa, may be in for one or two surprises. A careful scrutiny of one or two of the more detailed advertisements should make this clear. The full range of possibilities is indicated in 'Our villa selection in France is unbeatable: beachside villas with pools, a Loire chateau, and even a XVIth century Presidial in the Dordogne. Also caravans and holiday tents' (advertisement by Holiday Villas Ltd, *Sunday Telegraph*, 23 Jan 1983). If a 'villa' ranges from a Loire chateau at one end of the scale to a tent at the other, it is certainly an elastic item. One is bound to wonder how many of the 'hundreds of beautifully kept villas a pebble's throw from the beach' (advertisement by Beach Villas Ltd., *The Daily*

Telegraph, 23 Jan 1983) bear any resemblance to 'villas', in the tradi-tional sense of the word.

Virile

Creating a masculine image. *See also* DISCREET. The makers of what are beautifully called male toiletries face great and perhaps insuperable problems in finding adjectives which can be kept under proper control. The technique of selling perfume to women is very well understood and there is never the slightest danger that by using perfume a woman is going to cause anyone to believe that she is a lesbian. The reverse is in fact the case. With men, however, the situation is entirely different. The traditional attitude is that perfume indicates effeminacy at best and homosexuality at worst. It is therefore essential to discover adjectives which give precisely the opposite impression, a far from easy task. Dior has recently been experimenting with an interesting trio, 'Eau Sauvage. Virile. Discreet' (*New Yorker*, 14 June 1982). What 'Eau Sauvage' means is anybody's guess. It could be 'Wild Water', it could be 'The Water of Savages', not a very appealing thought. Whatever it is, the untamed, brute image is what is being striven for. 'Discreet' has been discussed above, and there remains 'virile'.

It could mean 'strong', but this seems unlikely, partly because perfumes are supposed to be subtle, not strong, and partly because 'strong' would conflict with 'discreet'. It must therefore imply 'the essence of masculinity', but what on earth is that? The aroma of a rugger club changing-room, perhaps? There are other unpublishable possibili-ties, but Dior does, after all, have its exalted name to consider.

Visible

Important? Presentable? To be used as a spokesman? The industrial and commercial worlds are populated by two distinct races of people. The master-race is small in number, but allowed and encouraged to be seen by the public. Its members are 'visible'. The proles, the toiling masses, on the other hand, must never be noticed, at least as individuals. They are 'invisible'. To point to someone, therefore, as 'This highly visible and integral team member' (*Boston Globe*, 11 Oct 1981) is to label him officer-class, one of the elite.

Vital

(*i*) Essential, all important; (*ii*) living. It is useful to be sure of which of these two meanings is intended. Otherwise, one could be bewildered by 'in-depth specialised discussions of the vital issues of death and dying' mailing by Baywood Publishing Company, Farmingdale, New York, 1981). Only somewone with an academic's or a businessman's lack of a sense of humour could cobble up a sentence like this and most diseased language owes its character to this more than to any other cause. To be able to find meaningless nonsense funny is to be inoculated against it.

W

Ways

Habits. For some unexplained reason, 'ways' is a classier word than 'habits' among social anthropologists and social scientists generally. One finds it in such contexts as 'Patterns in Urban Food Ways: an Example for Early Twentieth Century Atlanta (catalogue, Academic Press, New York, 1982). This supposed superiority of 'ways' over 'habits' is probably caused by a feeling that 'habit' is slightly patronizing or derogatory, that is, it indicates an attitude on the part of the observer, a 'value-judgement', which the true scholar must avoid at all costs. 'Ways', by contrast, is objective, pure, uncontaminated by personal prejudice. There is, of course, no need to fall in with some absurdities, but it is as well to be aware of them.

Wealth

Much. For years one has been poking gentle fun at house agents and hotels for the 'wealth of oak beams', which almost reached the point of being a compound noun. In more recent years, 'wealth' has moved away a little from the oak beams and attached itself to other favourites in the agents' pocket dictionary. 'Character' is one of them. A house in Sussex, for instance, is offered 'with a wealth of character' (*Sunday Telegraph*, 6 June 1982). 'Wealth' is an invaluable word, suggesting as it does not only quantity by quality as well. 'Lots of character' would not do at all.

Wearable

Not extreme, not tight-fitting, practical. This is a great favourite among those whose business it is to sell the more expensive kinds of clothes. One therefore has 'a natural cowhide European-styled wallet that's exquisitely slim and elegantly wearable' (*New Yorker*, 14 June 1982), and an 'extraordinarily wearable tie' (*New Yorker*, 7 June 1982). By implication, there must be a great many clothes being bought and worn which are not 'wearable' at all and one has only to use one's eyes to be convinced that this is indeed so. 'Wearable' clothes are always the ones

151

which are most difficult to buy, mainly because there is less profit in them.

Welcome

Accept. There is an American myth, now much in evidence elsewhere, that every Hilton, Sheraton and the rest is run just as if it were a small, 19th century family concern, with mine host waiting at the door with a friendly smile of greeting. This has, unfortunately, little foundation in fact, but it is a pleasant enough fiction, encouraged by the extensive use of the magic word, 'welcome'. So anxious are visitors — 'guests' — to be 'welcomed', that is, to be treated as individuals, and so willing are the hotels to oblige them, that not only they but everything belonging to them is now officially 'welcomed'. Thomas Cook will say of their traveller's cheques, for instance, 'They're known and welcomed at prestigious establishments' (*New Yorker*, 17 May 1982). They are, in fact, 'accepted', but to use such a cold, clinical term would be to remove oneself automatically from the company of decent hotel-keepers. The traveller's cheque itself, of course, is completely indifferent as to whether it is 'welcomed' or 'accepted'. *See also* GUEST.

We're

We are. During the 1970s those who scan the job advertisements closely will have noticed the growth of the very unpleasant habit of beginning the piece with 'We're', instead of 'We are', in order to give a chatty, democratic flavour to one's requirements. The results of this pathetic attempt are easy to illustrate. 'We're King Wilkinson, one of the world's most respected international Project Service Consultants' (*The Daily Telegraph*, 18 Dec 1981) says one organization, while from another comes 'We're looking for a technical sales person with three years expert sales experience' (*The Daily Telegraph*, 11 Dec 1981). The second example begins its next sentence, 'You'll...', which is a move in the same direction. There is no reason to be taken in by this nonsense. It is the industrial equivalent of murderous dictators being filmed as they pat babies on the head and saying how fond they are of dogs.

West Country

From, made in, typical of the West Country of England. There is no precise definition of the 'West Country'. Some would include Somerset, some Dorset, and there are even those empire builders who would tack on Gloucestershire. But everyone would agree that Devon and Cornwall are in the 'West Country', that great caricature of rural

England, where the sun always shines, the grass is always green, the whole population eats clotted cream three times a day, and accents can be cut with a knife. It is possible, however, to speak of the 'West Country' in ways which are not strictly honest and this, alas, happens with increasing frequency. A processor and supplier of meat, for example, will tell prospective customers that 'Its beautiful West Country taste is captured in our special vacuum-sealed packs' (*The Daily Telegraph*, 23 Sept 1982). There is, alas, no such thing as a 'West Country taste', in meat or anything else. If a panel of experts were to be confronted with half-a-dozen cooked samples of the same kind of meat, each from a different part of the country and including one from Devon or Cornwall, they would be extremely lucky to place even one in its correct county of origin. In the consumer's interest, it is more than time that this West Country bluff was called. *See also* FARMHOUSE.

Whole
Heads, tails and all. 'Whole wheat' and 'whole food' we know — 'The old Bakehouse, Whole Food Shop' (over front of shop in Castle Cary, Somerset, and widely elsewhere) — and there is broad agreement as to what they mean. But 'Whole Prawn Salad' (menu, Great Northern Hotel, London, July 1982) is a different matter. The salad presumably contains prawns in the plural — one can hardly be offered just one whole prawn, unless it is a prawn of quite unprecedented size — but exactly how much of each little creature is a 'whole prawn', with or without the capital letters? Is it the complete prawn, shell, whiskers, head and all, or the prawn, entire and unmutilated, as removed from its shell? Some eaters might be willing to order one, but not the other. They could, of course, ask the waitress, but why should they have to? There should by now be a legally approved definition of a Whole Prawn.

Will
Does. The package tour industry is constructed around the word 'will'. The Americans began it and the British in the same line of business have taken to it like ducks to water. The flavour in the USA and in the UK is not the same, however. In the UK, to say 'You will do this or that' sounds brusque and suggests that one is being given orders, whereas in the USA it is much more of a simple future. 'Your stay will include three days and two nights in the magnificent Pinehurst Hotel', say the *New York Times*, (2 Sept 1981), to which the true-born Englishman, but not the American, would traditionally respond, 'Who's pushing me around and telling me what to do?' By now, however, after reading his proper ration of travel

brochures each year, the holiday veteran has been hit over the head so often by 'will' that he has become anaesthetized and hardly notices it any more. The new recruit to the ranks may bristle for a while, though, as he finds himself ordered about by such sentences as 'Now you will swim, sunbathe and enjoy the tropical atmosphere' (Jetsave brochure, *USA and Canada*, April-Oct 1983). He is back at school or in the army.

Worker writers

Part-time writers. 'Worker' was dealt with thoroughly in *The Dictionary of Diseased English* and there is nothing of any significance to add here. But the new phrase, 'worker writer' does seem to call for some comment. These people now have their own organization, the 'Federation of worker writers and community publishers' (on the Federations's *List of Member Groups*, 1980). A careful examination of the Federation's literature suggests that the people who are members nearly all have jobs — this makes them 'workers', even if the jobs are of a strongly middle-class type — and write in their spare time. People have been doing this at least since the days of Chaucer, but nobody seems to have thought of Chaucer, Pepys, Milton, Lamb and Trollope as 'worker writers'.

The fact is that, in order to qualify for this label, one must belong to some sort of organization, in order to 'share experiences' and one's political and social opinions must be well to the left of centre. One must be trying to advance a common cause. 'Worker writers' have quite a lot in common with the 'worker priests'. Both share the philosophy that one writes or saves souls 'better' if one does it from the solid base of a job. A writer can, like Balzac, work 20 hours a day and a parish priest can toil from dawn to dusk on behalf of his flock but, so strange and perverse is today's terminology, that neither would qualify as a 'worker'. Tell that, one is tempted to say, to the bees. 'Worker writers', it should be noted, do not have 'meetings', which are bourgeois. They have 'workshops'.

Working people

Members of trade unions. The phrase has been carefully nursed and promoted by the trade unions and the political left for many years, as an essential part of the great fairy story by which the adult population of capitalist countries is permanently and inevitably divided into two halves, those who exploit and those who are exploited. Members of the professions, small shopkeepers and other self-employed people, are not 'working people', even though they may work twice as hard as those who officially are. 'Working people' is not, in fact, an objective description of any section of society, nor is it meant to be. It is a highly emotive term, used by people who earn their living from political organizations and, as such, it cannot be subjected to the ordinary rules of grammer, logic or common sense, as the British Communist Party's daily newspaper makes clear when it castigates a new government measure as having been brought in 'to boost the burden on working people' (*Morning Star*, 5 Nov 1981).

World class
Of a good international standard. 'World class' was invented by American advertisers in the late 1970s. It is a little masterpiece of nonsense and the extent to which it has been taken up, both inside and outside the USA, is proof of its brilliance. 'First class' had had its day. It was socially divisive, there were not enough people who were able or willing to pay for it, and there was a feeling of yesterday gathering around it. 'World class' suffers from none of these drawbacks and it has the added priceless advantage of meaning absoulutely nothing at all. Pressed hard to explain it, the hotels, shops, restaurants and transport undertakings who use it would probably come up with some such answer as 'patronized by the very best people, independent of place or nationality'. Inspection of the product leaves one in some doubt, however, as to whether this blanket commendation is in fact justified. One should be very careful indeed of anything which describes itself as 'world class'. It will certainly be both expensive and, up to a point, snobbish, but nothing else about it can be guaranteed. 'World class' is assuredly not the same as 'first class'. But it pulls in the customers and it is profitable, and what else can one ask of a word? A little anthology of 'world class', with the right kind of drawings, would be a pleasant Christmas present. It might include such cameos as 'World class dining' (*New Yorker*, 17 May 1982), the Royal Viking Line's 'On board ship, of course, the elegance is World Class' (*London Portrait*, Jan 1983) and, invaluable to all seekers after the Good Life, 'Where to dine World Class' (*New Yorker*, 17 May 1982).

A note on sources

As I explained in the Introduction, *The Dictionary of Even More Diseased English* carries on where its predecessor left off. The major offenders have not mended their ways and some are committing even worse crimes today than five or ten years ago. But a work of this kind cannot offer more than a selection of villainies and absurdities. The intention has been to show how one person has, in the interests of civilization and humanity, hacked his own way through the jungle of lies, half-truths, pomposities and misleading statements which make up such a large part of public English today. An instinct for self-preservation has admittedly played some part in this campaign, but my weapons are there for all to use.

This new *Dictionary*, like the first, concentrates on identifying the enemy, in his many forms, and on bringing him to trial. Essentially, the enemy is always the same — the person who has little or nothing of any value to sell, but who, in order to earn a living, has to pretend otherwise, the confidence trickster to whom the foolish and the innocent give a licence to operate. Because this is a personal book, I have, not unreasonably, I hope, taken my examples from publications which I read regularly or which have come easily to hand in the course of my travels. Others, I hope, will do exactly the same. I should like to make it as clear as I can that I have no reason whatever to believe that 'my' sources contain, issue by issue, a particularly dreadful or heavy crop of Diseased English. Had I, for example, combed the current literature of architecture and town planning, football or high fashion, I am sure I could have made a second collection as frightening as the first. But, moving in my own world, I have relied on the following:

Newspapers — all published in London, unless another place is specified, in the title or in brackets after it:

Birmingham Post, The
Boston Globe

157

A note on sources

Bristol Evening Post
Daily Express
Daily Telegraph, The
Edinburgh Evening News
Financial Times
Guardian, The
Morning Star
New Standard
New York Times
Scotsman (Edinburgh)
Sunday Telegraph
Sunday Times, The
Times, The
Western Gazette (Yeovil)

Periodicals

American Journal of Psychiatry
American Psychologist
American Sociological Review
British Journal of Psychiatry
British Psychological Bulletin (London)
Country Life (London)
Garden, The (London)
London Portrait
London Property
New Musical Express (London)
Newsletter of the Society of Architectural Historians
  (Washington, DC)
New Society
New Yorker
New York Review of Books
Screw West (Los Angeles)
Swissair Gazette

Occasional publications — these are fully identified in the text.

Restaurant and café menus

The name and place are given in the text. There would almost certainly be legal problems if one were to attempt to describe the level and quality of the establishment. Readers must be left to follow the clues provided.

Broadcasting

All the references are to BBC Radio 4 programmes. For those who are unfamiliar with the organization of BBC Radio, it may be helpful to know that BBC 1 and 2 are lowbrow, BBC 3 is highbrow, and BBC 4 is middlebrow.